Seasons of Celebrations

with

THE HAPPY COOKing LADY

A Collection of Recipes and Memories

from

Christine De Los Santos

Happy Cooking!

Copyright © 2018 Christine De Los Santos

All rights reserved. No part of this book may be reproduced or transmitted in any form or by any means, electronic or mechanical, including: photocopying, recording, or by any information storage and retrieval system, without permission in writing from the copyright owners.

Seasons of Celebrations with the Happy Cooking Lady:
A Collection of Recipes and Memories

Recipes from Christine De Los Santos

Food Styling and Photographs by Joel De Los Santos

Edited by Lyda Rose Haerle & Griffin Mill

Cover and Interior Design & Layout by Michael Nicloy

Cover and Interior Author Images:
Photos by Mamee Laufer
Frame Me by Mamee Photography, Oshkosh, WI

Hair by Sue Gahlman; Makeup by Shaina Lindberg
Hair Extraordinaire, Green Bay, WI

ISBN 978-1945907357

BISAC Codes:

CKB 000000 COOKING | General
CKB 07700 COOKING | Seasonal
CKB127000 COOKING | Comfort Food

Published by Nico 11 Publishing & Design
www.nico11publishing.com

Be well read.

Quantity order requests can be emailed to:
mike@nico11publishing.com

Printed in the United States of America

Table of Contents

Introduction   11

Spring   13

  Asparagus & Rhubarb Harvest Time   14
    Asparagus Crab Dip   15
    Bacon-Wrapped Asparagus   16
    Asparagus Mushroom Quiche   17
    Rhubarb Coffee Cake   18
    Rhubarb Crisp   19
    Mom's Rhubarb Muffins   20
    Rhubarb Jam   21

  Valentine's Day   22
    Wild Rice with Mushrooms and Almonds   23
    Cherry Fudge   24
    Peanut Butter Hearts   25
    Chocolate Meringue Shells   26
    Mocha Soufflés   27
    Cake for Two   28

  Saint Patrick's Day   29
    Asparagus Soup   30
    Reuben Bake   31
    Leprechaun Shake   32
    Chocolate Mint Torte   33
    Chocolate Mint Truffles   34

  Easter   35
    My Favorite Easter Memory   36
    Easter Lamb   37
    Ham Glaze   38
    Hot Mustard   39
    My Deviled Eggs   40
    Leftover Holiday Soup   41
    Carrot Cake Cookies with
      Cream Cheese Frosting   42
    Easter Nests   44

  Baby & Bridal Showers   45
    Springtime Cake   46
    Rose Cupcakes   47
    Party Popcorn Mix   48
    Baby Shower Twinkies   49
    Baby Face Cupcakes   50
    Baby Buggy Deviled Eggs   51
    Homemade Butter Mints   52

Summer 55

Summer Fruits 56
- Raspberry Cream Cheese Muffins 57
- Mom's Cherry Cobbler 58
- Cherry Pie 59
- Banana Raspberry Bread 60
- Lemony Raspberry Muffins 61
- Belgian Waffles 62
- Blueberry French Toast Bake 63

Garden Goodies 64
- Zucchini Nut Loaf 65
- Crispy Zucchini Spears 66
- Shrimp with Zucchini and Tomatoes 67
- Chicken with Summer Squash 68
- Grandma's Cucumber Salad 69
- Chocolate Zucchini Cake 70
- Cabbage with Italian Sausage 71
- Pickled Beets 72
- Dilly Beans 73
- Pickled Banana Peppers 74

Summer Celebrations 75
- A 4th of July Memory 76
- The perfect No-Cook 4th of July Breakfast 77
- My Potato Salad 78
- Grandma B's Baked Beans 79
- Grandma B's German Potato Salad 80
- Crispy Cole Slaw 81
- Broccoli Salad 82
- Asian Cole Slaw 83

Fall 85

Apples 86
- Apple Pie 87
- Apple Raspberry Crisp 88
- Crockpot Apple Butter 89
- Grandma's Apple Slab Cake 90
- Apple Cinnamon Smoothie 92
- Caramel Apple Bread Pudding 93

Pumpkins 94
- Pumpkin Chipotle Pasta Sauce 95
- Pumpkin Zucchini Cranberry Bread 96
- Roasted Pumpkin Seeds 97
- Turtle Pumpkin Pie 98
- Pumpkin Tiramisu 99

Pumpkin Torte	100
Pumpkin Cake Roll	101
Pumpkin Butter	102
Soups	**103**
Potato Sausage Soup	104
Wild Rice Mushroom Soup	105
Beefy Tomato Mushroom Soup	106
Calico Bean Soup	107
Curried Carrot Soup	108
Butternut Squash Soup	109
Minestrone Soup	110
Pumpkin, Barley, and Sage Soup	111
Pasta	**112**
Enjoy Those Fresh Tomatoes! Pasta	113
Butternut Squash Mac & Cheese	114
Butternut Squash Ravioli	115
Pasta with Italian Sausage and Vegetable Sauce	116
Italian Pasta Bake	117
Mary's Pasta Salad	118
Football Season	**119**
Cheesy Football	120
Chili	121
Meatballs in Football (Snap)py Sauce	122
Krispie Football Field	123
Cinnamon Orange Snack Mix	124
Halloween	**125**
Blood, Worm, and Eyeball Soup	126
Monster Mash with Fingers	127
Ghosts & Monster Smiles	128
Halloween Deviled Eggs	129
Orange Jack-O-Lantern Cookies	129
Thanksgiving	**130**
Recipe for Laughter	131
Candied Sweet Potatoes	132
Crescent Rolls	133
Green Fluffy Stuff	134
Wild Rice and Cranberry Bread	135
Stuffing Waffles	136

Winter — 139

Christmas Cookies and Desserts — 140
- Grandma's Gingerbread Folks — 141
- Three Ribbon Cookies — 142
- Snickerdoodles — 143
- Almond Thumbprints — 144
- Cranberry-Orange Biscotti — 145
- Eggnog Crème Brûlée — 146
- Graham Cracker Torte — 147
- Sweet Potato Pie — 148

Christmas Gifts and Candy — 149
- A Christmas Memory — 150
- Oyster Dillies — 151
- Cinnamon Pecans — 152
- Brown Bread — 153
- Peanut Butter Fudge — 154
- Mom's Best Fudge — 155
- Aloha Fudge — 156

Year-Round Family Foods — 159

Veggies — 160
- Vegetarian Enchiladas — 161
- Ravioli with Chickpeas and Veggies — 162
- Fried Corn — 163
- Cajun Sweet Potatoes — 164
- Baked Breaded Eggplant — 165
- Grilled Veggie Medley — 166
- Stuffed Acorn Squash — 167

Chicken, Beef, and Pork — 168
- Chicken Tostadas with Black Bean Salsa — 169
- Chicken Fajitas — 170
- Chicken Curry in the Slow Cooker — 171
- Italian Meatballs — 172
- Souper Burgers — 173
- Hubby's Easy Enchiladas — 174
- Stuffed Peppers — 175
- Cindy's Surprise Casserole — 176
- Slow Cooker Pot Roast — 177
- Baked Pork Chops — 178

Seafood — 179
- Our Favorite Tuna Casserole — 180
- Salmon with Tangy Dill Sauce — 181
- Seafood Stew — 182
- Shrimp with Veggies — 183

Quick Shrimp Fried Rice	184
Jamaican Shrimp and Rice	185
Shrimp Tacos	186
Cajun Shrimp with Sausage Skillet	187
Basics	188
Pie Crust	189
Home-Baked Croutons	190
Crockpot Stock	191
Desserts	192
Marble Cake Memory	193
Bananas Foster	194
Lemon Raspberry Cheesecake Bars	195
Blender Chocolate Mousse	196
Nunnie's Sour Cream Coffee Cake	197
Orange Sugar Cookies	198
Mom's Super Simple Doughnuts	199
Diane's Famous Chocolate Chip, Oatmeal, Cranberry, Walnut Cookies	200
Mom's Chocolate Yeast Cake	201
Sugar Cut-Out Cookies	202
My Vanilla Sugar Cookie Frosting	203

About the Author   207

Introduction

If I have ever cooked or baked for you, it means that I think you are wonderful, and I am happy that you are a part of my life. That is how it works with me. Food is my language of love and friendship, the way that I show that I care…good, old-fashioned comfort food, nothing too fancy, nothing too difficult, no oddball ingredients.

I believe in the 3 C's of recipes: Collect, Change, Create. If I find a recipe that works well and needs no changes, that is one that I Collect. If I know who gave it to me originally, they get the credit. Sometimes I find a recipe that just needs a couple of Changes to adapt to my family's personal tastes. Then, there are the recipes that sometimes just get Created, with a little of this, a little of that, and with those wonderful "leftovers" that are given a new life. Don't be afraid to have some fun in the kitchen. Enjoy Collecting, Changing, and Creating.

During my lifetime, I have been blessed with knowing many good cooks, even great ones. My mom knew how to stretch the most out of a food budget, as did my grandmothers. Baking has always been a part of our family history (my Great-Grandpa was a baker by trade), especially with seasonal ingredients from our family gardens and orchards. My memories include heading to Aunt Gertie's farm to pick pears, or to Aunt Cora's to pick raspberries. I remember sitting on the roof of my grandparents' garage to pick cherries that were too high to reach from the ground. Rhubarb was something that almost all of my relatives grew. Then, there was the plum bush that was so heavy with fruit every year that we had to prop up the branches with the wooden poles that mom usually used to prop up the laundry lines, when they were heavy with clothes. Mom spent hours peeling apples from our apple trees at home, and making grape jam from the grapes in our yard. Those are the cooks that I learned from.

In my adult life, my husband Joel introduced me to Mexican food. I had never so much as tasted an avocado, let alone had a homemade tortilla. What an awakening! My best girlfriend Jean Rohr and I have cooked so many wonderful lunches for each other. We wanted to try recipes that our husbands might not eat. Turns out that they did, especially the desserts. My friend Amy Hanten introduced me to cooking on TV, and started me on a whole new chapter of cooking.

One of our greatest joys for Joel and me as a couple is opening up our home every other Sunday to our kids and grandchildren for a family meal. Whoever can make it is welcomed, and fed well. Plus the holidays…how can you celebrate a holiday without great food? I don't believe that it can be done, and don't even want to try.

This Cookbook was originally intended to be a gift for my family members and friends, to catalog family recipes so they would not be lost. The project grew. My wonderful husband Joel photographed all of my recipes. I am not a professional food stylist, nor is he a professional photographer. These pictures are how I normally would serve these dishes. I am a collector of dishes and table linen, sometimes to a fault, and these photos gave me a chance to use them just a little bit more.

My hope is that you will use some of my recipes to show the people that you love and care about how you feel about them. Enjoying a meal with people you love, taking treats to a treasured neighbor, making food for someone having a hard time…food is a universal language that we all can speak.

Speak it well, and make someone *Happy*.

My Great-Grandpa was a baker. Here is his delivery truck. I did not know about this part of my family history until I found this photo…long after I had started my own bakery. It proves that baking is in my blood.

Spring

Asparagus & Rhubarb Harvest Time...14
Valentine's Day...22
Saint Patrick's Day...29
Easter...35
Baby & Bridal Showers...45

Asparagus & Rhubarb Harvest Time

Asparagus Crab Dip...15
Bacon-Wrapped Asparagus....16
Asparagus Mushroom Quiche...17
Rhubarb Coffee Cake...18
Rhubarb Crisp...19
Mom's Rhubarb Muffins...20
Rhubarb Jam...21

Asparagus Crab Dip

This is a wonderful hot dip, but also tastes great once it has cooled to room temperature as well.

- **12-14** stalks of asparagus, depending upon thickness
- **½ Cup** sour cream, light will work just fine
- **1** 8-oz. block of cream cheese, softened (light is just fine to use)
- **½ Cup** grated Parmesan cheese
- **2 tsp.** mustard with horseradish
- **2** green onions, chopped, both white and green part
- **1** 6-oz. can of crab meat, no need to use the expensive kind, drained or ½ Cup chopped artificial crab meat
- **½ Cup** sliced almonds

Preheat oven to 375°.

After breaking off the tough ends of the asparagus, steam or boil until very soft.

Drain if boiling.

Chop into small pieces.

In a medium bowl, mix the asparagus, sour cream and cream cheese until well blended.

Add the cheese, mustard, onion and crab meat. (Please note that if using the artificial crab meat, it might not be gluten free.)

Spread evenly into a 1 quart baking dish. Sprinkle almonds on top.

Bake for 20-25 minutes until bubbly and heated through.

To make ahead:

If you would like to make this ahead of time, it could be put together the night before, minus the almonds.

Cover and refrigerate.

Pull the dish out of the refrigerator about 30 minutes before you want to bake it, then top with the almonds.

You might have to bake for an additional 5 minutes or so.

Serve with crackers, fresh vegetables, or tortilla chips.

Bacon-Wrapped Asparagus

This is a wonderful side dish for anything from pork chops to chicken. It's great with steak as well. Having an abundance of asparagus growing in the garden, it is always great to have new ways to use it.

For each serving:
3-4 medium stalks of asparagus, tough ends removed
1 thin piece of bacon
olive oil, pepper, grated Parmesan cheese

Preheat oven to 350°.
Line a baking pan with foil or parchment to make cleanup much easier.
Wrap the asparagus stalks together in the piece of bacon.
Brush the exposed tips with just a touch of olive oil.
Sprinkle with a little pepper.
Bake until the bacon is crispy. Sprinkle with a little Parmesan cheese.

Asparagus Mushroom Quiche

I save some of my Easter ham in the freezer just so I can make this dish once the garden starts producing asparagus.

1	9 inch ready-made deep dish pie crust, or a homemade deep dish pie crust (see: Basics, page 189)
8 oz.	button mushrooms, cleaned and chopped
1 tsp.	butter, margarine, or olive oil
3-4 oz.	Swiss cheese, diced
8 oz	cooked ham, diced
⅔ Cup	chopped fresh asparagus
1 Tblsp.	dried dill weed
1 Cup	heavy cream
5	large eggs

just a pinch of salt and pepper

Preheat oven to 350°.

Bake the pie crust for about 10 minutes.

Saute the mushrooms in the butter, margarine, or oil until they are soft and a lot of the liquid is released. Drain on paper towels to get the rest of the liquid out.

Mix the drained mushrooms, cheese, ham, asparagus, and dill together, then spoon into the partially-baked pie crust.

Whisk the cream, eggs, salt, and pepper together until well blended.

Pour over the mixture that is already in the crust. Bake for about an hour. Check when that time is almost up to see if the middle is set. It should not jiggle when moved. It is done when it is firm to the touch in the middle.

Let set for about 15 minutes before slicing.

This freezes well and reheats well from refrigerated state in either the microwave or oven.

Rhubarb Coffee Cake

This makes a nice 9 by 13 inch pan of a wonderful, moist coffee cake.

Makes 16-20 servings.

1½ Cups	sugar
½ Cup	butter or margarine, softened
2	eggs
2 tsp.	vanilla
2 Cups	all-purpose flour
1 tsp.	baking soda
2 tsp.	ground cinnamon
1 Cup	buttermilk
4 Cups	frozen or fresh rhubarb (if using frozen, measure while frozen, then thaw and drain in colander, but do not press liquid out)

Topping:

½ Cup	packed brown sugar
1 Cup	all-purpose flour
1 tsp.	ground cinnamon
½ Cup	cold butter, but in small cubes

Preheat oven to 350°

In a large bowl, cream the sugar and softened butter or margarine until light and fluffy. Add eggs, one at a time, beating well. Beat in vanilla.

Combine dry ingredients; add to the creamed mixture. Stir in buttermilk, then rhubarb. Pour into greased 9 by 13 inch baking dish (non-metal).

In a small bowl, combine the first 3 topping ingredients. Cut in butter until mixture looks like coarse crumbs. Sprinkle over batter.

Bake for 45-55 minutes, or until toothpick inserted near center comes out clean.

Cool in pan on wire rack.

This recipe can be cut in half and baked in an 8 inch pan, if desired

Rhubarb Coffee Cake (left) with Asparagus Mushroom Quiche (right).

Rhubarb Crisp

Topping:
- 1 Cup flour
- ½ Cup oatmeal
- 1 Cup brown sugar, packed
- ½ Cup melted margarine

Filling:
- 4 Cups chopped rhubarb (or combination of rhubarb and strawberries, 3 parts rhubarb to 1 part strawberries)
- 1 Cup sugar
- ¼ Cup flour
- ½ tsp. ground cinnamon
- ½ Cup water

Preheat oven to 375°.

Mix first 3 topping ingredients, add margarine, mix well.

Lightly grease 8 by 8 inch pan.

Put filling ingredients into pan and mix well. Lightly pat on topping.

Bake uncovered 35-45 minutes until golden brown and rhubarb is soft. If using frozen rhubarb, you might not need to add the water, as once it defrosts, it contains excess water.

Serve with ice cream or whipped topping.

If you want to use a 9 by 13 inch pan, just double the recipe.

Mom's Rhubarb Muffins

I was fortunate to live in two houses growing up, and both had a wonderful abundance of rhubarb growing in the yard.

Makes 24 muffins

1½ Cups	brown sugar, firmly packed
1 Cup	buttermilk
⅔ Cup	vegetable oil
1	egg
2½ Cups	all-purpose flour
1 tsp.	baking soda
1 tsp.	salt
1 tsp.	vanilla
1½ Cups	rhubarb, chopped in small pieces (can use frozen, thawed, chopped rhubarb)
½ Cup	chopped nuts (I like pecan or walnut), optional

Preheat oven to 350°.
In a large bowl, mix the brown sugar, buttermilk, oil, and egg until smooth.
Add flour, baking soda, salt, and vanilla.
Blend well, but do not over beat.
Stir in the rhubarb and nuts.
Pour batter into muffin cups in a muffin tin, or a greased muffin tin.
Fill about ½ full.

Mix topping:

½ Cup	sugar
1 Tblsp.	butter

Blend with fork until crumbly. Sprinkle each muffin with some of the sugar topping. Bake for 30-40 minutes until a toothpick comes out clean.
I like to individually wrap and freeze some of these.
They freeze great.

Rhubarb Jam

Mom still makes this jam, as she always has an abundance of rhubarb growing. It is very easy and inexpensive to make.

10 Cups rhubarb cut into ¼ inch pieces
5 Cups sugar
2 3-oz. (4 serving size) packages of strawberry gelatin

Put rhubarb, then sugar in a covered plastic bowl overnight in refrigerator. No need to stir.

Put the rhubarb and sugar mixture into a large kettle, as well as any liquid that has collected in the bowl.

Bring to a boil over medium heat.

Boil for 20 minutes, on low. Stir frequently.

Stir in the gelatin when it is done boiling, while mixture is still hot.

Make sure gelatin is dissolved.

You can either store this in jars in the refrigerator, or freeze in plastic containers.

Valentine's Day

Wild Rice with Mushrooms and Almonds...23
Cherry Fudge...24
Peanut Butter Hearts...25
Chocolate Meringue Shells...26
Mocha Soufflés...27
Cake for Two...28

Wild Rice with Mushrooms and Almonds

We have this with our home cooked Valentine's Day dinner, but it is good any time. It cooks in the oven, so you can cook along side a roast, chicken, whatever you are having. Our usual is Cornish hens.

Makes four ½ cup servings, recipe can be doubled if needed.

2 Tblsp.	butter or margarine
4 oz.	button mushrooms, cleaned and sliced
¼ Cup	slivered almonds
½ Cup	wild rice, uncooked
¼ Cup	green onions, sliced
2 Cups	chicken or beef stock, depending upon your main dish or preference

Preheat oven to 350°. Grease a 1½ quart baking dish.

Melt butter or margarine in a large skillet over medium heat.

Add mushrooms and almonds, cook and stir until mushrooms are tender and almonds are beginning to brown.

Add wild rice and cook for about 10 minutes, stirring often.

Add onions and broth, bring to a boil.

Pour into greased baking dish.

Bake for 45 minutes covered, then an additional 45-60 minutes uncovered until rice is tender and liquid is absorbed.

Cherry Fudge

This is such a simple recipe, but makes a nice batch of tasty fudge in minutes.

1   12-oz. bag of white chocolate chips
1   16-oz. can of cherry flavored frosting, not the whipped kind

edible pink glitter, if desired.
⅓ Cup   **semisweet chocolate chips, if desired**
½ tsp.   **shortening, if doing a chocolate drizzle**

Spray a 9 by 9 inch pan with cooking spray.
In a double boiler, or carefully in the microwave in a medium-sized bowl, melt the white chocolate chips.
Once the chips are melted, remove from heat and stir the frosting into the melted chips until completely blended.
Scoop into the prepared pan, leveling the top with a spoon or spatula so it is spread evenly.
Sprinkle with the edible glitter if desired.
Refrigerate for about 30 minutes and cut into squares. You might want to use a heart-shaped cookie cutter to cut out a heart or two.
If you want to do a chocolate drizzle over the fudge, separate the pieces of fudge and put on a wax paper or parchment lined work area.
Melt the chocolate chips and shortening together in the microwave.
Using a butter knife, drizzle the melted chocolate over the fudge.

Other options: add about ¼ tsp. of almond extract to the fudge after mixing the white chocolate chips with the frosting.
Chopped nuts could also be added, ⅓ cup.

Peanut Butter Hearts

These are a wonderful peanut butter cutout. They can also be cut out with a smaller-sized heart cutter and dipped half in chocolate, instead of the drizzle. I also use these cut-outs to do reindeer cookies at Christmas time. Just add a small red baking bit for the nose and a green one for the eye, attached with the melted chocolate, and then don't do the chocolate drizzle.

Number of cookies that this makes is dependent upon the size cutter you use.

1 Cup	peanut butter chips
½ Cup	butter or margarine
⅔ Cup	packed brown sugar
1	large egg
1 tsp.	vanilla
½ Cup	ground pecans
1⅓ Cup	all-purpose flour
¾ tsp.	baking soda

Preheat oven to 350°.
In a saucepan, heat the peanut butter chips and butter or margarine on low.
Stir constantly until both are melted.
Transfer to a large bowl.
Add the brown sugar and stir until all the lumps are out.
Add the egg and vanilla, stir until combined.
Add the pecans, flour, and baking soda. Mix well.
Spoon the dough onto a piece of plastic wrap, cover with the wrap, and chill in the refrigerator 15 minutes or so, until easy to handle.
Roll between 2 sheets of wax paper to about ¼ inch.
Cut out with cookie cutter and place on parchment lined baking sheets.
Bake for 7-9 minutes, depending upon size of cookie.
When done, they should be almost set in the middle.
Cool on pan 1 minute, then cool completely on a wire rack.
If doing a chocolate drizzle or dip on the cookies:
Put 1 cup of semisweet chocolate chips in a microwave-safe dish.
Add 1 tablespoon of shortening.
Heat in 15-second intervals in the microwave, stirring after each time.
This is done when nice and smooth.
Put the cooled cookies on a wax paper lined surface.
Using a butter knife, dip into the melted chocolate and drizzle small amounts over the cookies, doing this until desired appearance. This keeps large amounts of chocolate from drizzling at one time. Or, you can dip a smaller cookie halfway into the chocolate, then drip off excess and place on the wax paper to dry.

Chocolate Meringue Shells

A wonderful, lighter dessert to finish off your Valentine's Day meal.

3 egg whites at room temperature
¼ tsp. cream of tartar
¾ Cup granulated sugar
2 Tblsp. unsweetened cocoa powder

Preheat oven to 275°.
Line 2 baking sheets with parchment paper.
If you desire a shape other than round, draw shapes on the parchment paper (I do hearts).
Beat the egg whites with the cream of tartar until foamy.
Mix the sugar with the cocoa powder.
Add the sugar mixture to the egg whites a Tblsp. at a time.
Do not under beat. The mixture should end up thick and glossy.
Using a spoon, put mounds of the meringue on the prepared pans. Each one should use about ⅓ cup of the meringue.
Spread to a circle shape, or whatever shape you drew on the parchment.
Make sure to build up the outsides, there should be a lower portion in the middle for fillings.
Bake for 1 hour. Do not open up oven door.
Turn heat off and let set in oven for another 1½ hours.
Remove on parchment to a wire rack to cool completely.
Peel off parchment and store in a covered container.
You will get 8-9 meringues.
These can be filled with ice cream, pudding with berries, or whatever you like.
I like using a cherry filling with whipped cream for Valentine's day, and garnish with chocolate heart if desired. You can either use canned cherry pie filling, or my homemade cherry filling:

Cherry Filling:
2 Cups pitted tart cherries
You can use frozen, just defrost them first
No need to get rid of the juice
½ Cup + 2 Tblsp. granulated sugar
1½ Tblsp. cornstarch
⅛ tsp. almond extract, if desired, or vanilla
In a saucepan, mix the cherries, sugar, and cornstarch.
Cook over medium heat stirring constantly until mixture boils and thickens.
Turn heat down and cook for an additional minute, stirring constantly.
Remove from heat. Add almond or vanilla extract.

Chocolate Heart:
¼ Cup semisweet chocolate chips
Put chocolate chips in a small zipper food bag.
Heat in microwave in 15-second increments.
Squish the chocolate with your fingers until you see it is melted. This usually takes three 15-second trips into the microwave.
Cut a small hole in the corner of the bag. Pipe small heart shapes freehand onto wax paper, or squiggles if hearts are too hard to draw.
Put wax paper into refrigerator to harden up the chocolate.
Peel off and top off your dessert with this cute garnish.

Mocha Soufflés

*This impressive dessert is light and chocolaty, but easy to make.
It can be stored in the freezer until ready to bake, and you can bake just one at a time, if you like.
If you are like me and love the flavors of coffee and chocolate together, this one is for you!*

Nonstick cooking spray	
3	egg whites
2-3 tsp.	granulated sugar (to coat custard cups)
5 Tblsp. + 1 tsp.	granulated sugar
2 Tblsp.	all-purpose flour
½ tsp.	instant coffee granules, or instant espresso granules
2½ Tblsp.	semisweet chocolate chips
2 Tblsp.	unsweetened cocoa powder
a dash of	salt
1 Cup	fat-free evaporated milk
½ tsp.	vanilla
1/16 tsp.	cream of tartar, just a pinch
5 Tblsp.	granulated sugar
powdered sugar for garnish	
seedless raspberry preserves, if desired	
chocolate syrup, if desired	

Preheat oven to 350°.
Place egg whites in a large mixer bowl. Let sit for 30 minutes.
Spray 4 (6-oz.) or 6 (4-oz.) custard cups with nonstick spray.
In each cup, use ½ tsp. granulated sugar to coat the bottom and sides of each cup.
Whisk the 5 Tblsp. + 1 tsp. Granulated sugar, flour, coffee granules, chocolate chips, cocoa powder, and salt together in a saucepan.
Add the evaporated milk. Cook and stir over medium heat until mixture is thickened and bubbly.
Remove from heat, stir in vanilla.
Pour into a large bowl, cover with plastic wrap and cool completely.
Beat the room temperature egg whites and cream of tartar with electric mixer until soft peaks form.
Continue beating, adding 1 Tblsp. of the final 5 Tblsp. of granulated sugar at a time. Beat until stiff peaks form.
Fold egg white mixture into cooled chocolate mixture.
Divide among the prepared custard cups.
Cover and freeze for 2 hours or until firm. These must be frozen before baking.
Wrap in heavy foil and freeze for up to 3 weeks.
To bake:
Place the desired amount of custard cups containing the frozen mixture in a large baking pan.
Place pan in the oven and pour boiling water into pan around the cups to a 1 inch depth.
Bake for approximately 35 minutes, maybe less for a 4-oz. cup.
When done, souffle will be puffed over the top of the cup and a knife inserted near the center will come out clean.
Garnish each with ¼ tsp. of powdered sugar dusted over the top. (I use a small tea strainer to do this.) You can also drizzle a little raspberry preserves and chocolate syrup over the top.
Eat right away, as they start to fall once they begin to cool, but still taste yummy.

Cake for Two

Don't feel like baking? This is the recipe for you.
These cakes are pretty, tasty, and take very little time to make.

   Makes 2 mini cakes

4	spongecake cups (like the kind used for strawberry shortcake)
2 Tblsp.	lemon curd (found near the jams and jellies in the grocery store)
2 Tblsp.	fresh blueberries
1 Cup	frozen whipped topping, thawed
¼ Cup	powdered sugar
¼ Cup	almond slices, toasted

if desired, fresh mint for garnish

Place one spongecake cup on each of two plates, cup/well side up.

Fill each cup with 1 Tblsp. of the lemon curd.

Top the lemon curd with 1 layer of blueberries, reserving 4 to 6 for garnishing.

Cover the filled spongecake cups with the other 2 spongecake cups, cup/well side down, so that the top is the flat side.

Mix the thawed whipped topping with the powdered sugar.

Frost the top and sides with the whipped topping mixture.

Garnish with a few rows of the sliced almonds around the bottom.

Garnish with fresh mint, if desired, and 2 or 3 fresh blueberries on each.

Great to split one for a romantic dessert, or have one for each.

You can play with the fillings. I have done both white chocolate pudding and chocolate pudding in place of the lemon curd.

I have replaced the blueberries with raspberries and strawberries.

Come up with your own fun combos. This is more of a basic method.

Refrigerate before serving and if there are any leftovers.

Saint Patrick's Day

Asparagus Soup...30
Reuben Bake...31
Leprechaun Shake...32
Chocolate Mint Torte...33
Chocolate Mint Truffles...34

Asparagus Soup

This is a great way to use up the ends that you snap off to use the tops for another recipe, or use the whole spear, just don't use the woody white part at the end.

A wonderful soup to make when the asparagus harvest is in full swing, or as a special treat on Saint Patrick's Day.

Make 2 servings

2 Cups   asparagus (a great way to use up the ends that you snap off to use the tops for another recipe, or use the whole spear, just don't use the woody white part at the end)
1 Cup   chicken or vegetable broth
2 Tblsp. chopped onion
salt and pepper to taste
1 piece of rye bread and drizzle of olive oil, if you want a rye crouton for on top.

Chop the asparagus, put in a sauce pan. Add the broth and onion. Cover and simmer until asparagus is tender. Use an immersion blender to puree the soup in the pot, or let cool completely and puree in a blender.
Add salt and pepper to taste.

To add a shamrock crouton:
Cut a shamrock out of rye bread with a shamrock shaped cookie cutter, drizzle with olive oil, and bake in the oven at 325° until crispy, to use this wonderful soup as a Saint Patrick's Day dish.

This is a wonderful, light soup with lots of asparagus flavor. If you want to make it a little more hardy, add imitation crab chunks to it after it is pureed and just heat.

It's an easy recipe to multiply for a larger batch, and it freezes well.

Reuben Bake

A wonderful way to use some of your leftover corned beef, or corned beef from the deli.

Makes 4-6 servings

1	8-oz. tube of refrigerated crescent rolls, reduced fat can be used
8 slices	Swiss cheese, thin sliced and/or reduced fat can be used
½ lb.	thinly sliced corned beef, or turkey pastrami
¼ Cup	Thousand Island dressing, light dressing can be used
⅔ Cup	Sauerkraut, rinsed and well drained
1	egg, beaten well

Preheat oven to 375°.
Spray a 9 by 9 inch or 8 by 8 inch baking pan with cooking spray.
Unroll the tube of crescent rolls. Cut in half crosswise.
Press one of the 2 sections of dough into the bottom of the baking pan, pressing to seal seams and perforations.
Bake 8-10 minutes until golden brown.
Layer 4 slices of cheese evenly on top of the dough.
Layer the meat on top of the cheese.
Mix the Thousand Island dressing and sauerkraut together in a small bowl.
Spread the dressing mixture on top of the meat.
Top with the last 4 slices of Swiss cheese
Press the seams and perforations out of the remaining section of dough.
Place the remaining piece of dough on top of the other ingredients in the baking dish.
Brush with the beaten egg. You will probably have some egg left.
Bake 13-18 minutes until top crust is golden brown.
Let sit for about 5 minutes before slicing.

Leprechaun Shake

    Makes one nice-sized serving

1 Cup   milk of your choice (Cashew and Almond milk can also be used, sweetened or unsweetened).
½   frozen banana, cut into chunks
1 drop green food color
1 small drop mint extract (not peppermint), you can use more if desired, but taste first, the extract is strong.
sweetener of choice, as much as you would put in 1 glass of iced tea or cup of coffee. I use one packet of Stevia, but you can use any others, including sugar.
a few ice cubes
whipped topping, if desired

Put the first 5 ingredients into your blender and blend until no chunks of banana are left.
If you want it thicker, add ice cubes one at a time until you achieve the desired consistancy.
Top with whipped topping, if desired.

Chocolate Mint Torte

If you want a thicker layer of frosting, double the frosting recipe.

23 or so whole CHOCOLATE graham crackers
3 Cups cold low fat or fat free milk
2 packages (4 servings size each) white chocolate or vanilla-flavored instant pudding and pie filling mix (you can use sugar-free)
¼ - ½ tsp. mint extract (not peppermint), depending upon how strong of a mint flavor you want)
3-4 drops green food coloring
1 8-oz. container frozen whipped topping, thawed

Cocoa Frosting:
1 Tblsp. butter
2 Tblsp. unsweetened cocoa powder
2 Tblsp. + 1 tsp. low fat or skim milk
1 Cup powdered sugar
1¼ tsp. vanilla

Grease 13 by 9 inch baking dish with nonstick cooking spray.
Line bottom of pan with 2 cracker halves and 6 whole crackers. Set aside.
Whisk milk and pudding mixes 2 minutes in large bowl until thickened.
Whisk in extract and food coloring. Add more coloring if you want a darker green.
Fold in whipped topping. Spread half of the pudding mixture over graham crackers.
Top with 3 graham cracker halves and 6 whole crackers. Spread remaining pudding mixture over crackers. Repeat graham cracker layer.
Cover and refrigerate 2 hours.

Prepare cocoa frosting, spread frosting over graham crackers. Refrigerate over night.

To make cocoa frosting:
Melt butter in small saucepan. Stir in cocoa and milk until blended. Remove from heat. Stir in powdered sugar and vanilla.

Chocolate Mint Truffles

I don't remember where I got this recipe originally, but I love it! So easy.
You can make a whole batch for what just a couple would cost in a fancy chocolate shop.

Makes about 24

1	10-oz. package of mint chocolate chips, make sure they are the chocolate plus mint kind, some are only mint
⅓ Cup	whipping cream
¼ Cup	butter

chocolate sprinkles, green sprinkles, ground nuts, unsweetened cocoa (your choice of decor)

Melt chips with whipping cream and butter in a medium saucepan or double boiler over low heat.
Stir occasionally until chips and butter are melted.
Pour into a pie pan or square baking pan.
Refrigerate until fudgy, but soft, about 2 hours.
Line a baking pan with wax paper.
Shape about 1 Tblsp. of mixture into a ball.
If mixture has hardened, rolling the dough between your hands to form a ball will still work once your hands warm it up (do not microwave or reheat).
Make all of the balls and place on the wax paper.
Put your sprinkles, or whatever decor you are using in small bowls (ramekins are the perfect size).
Roll each ball again between your palms to soften outside and roll in your chosen decor until covered on all sides.
Place each in a small candy cup, or even small muffin cups.
Refrigerate. Can refrigerate for up to 3 days, then can be frozen for several weeks.

Easter

My Favorite Easter Memory...36
Easter Lamb...37
Ham Glaze...38
Hot Mustard...39
My Deviled Eggs...40
Leftover Holiday Soup...41
Carrot Cake Cookies with
 Cream Cheese Frosting...42
Easter Nests...44

My Favorite Easter Memory

Easter memory of the day. Every Good Friday, while grandma was alive; that was our special day. I usually had a job where I could take the day off, or had it as a holiday.

I always packed us a lunch and would head down to Milwaukee to see her.

One year, I asked her what she would like for lunch and she said, "I would like to try one of those BOAT sandwiches. I have never had one."

I finally figured out that she was talking about SUB sandwiches.

So, I brought her down her first Subway sandwich and her first Funyuns, along with some of my Bunny Face cookies. After eating her sandwich and Funyons, she was full, and said she would save the cookies for later.

When my mom got off of work and stopped by with her supper and to give her her meds, she noticed that Grandma had taken off the pink and blue M&M's that I use to decorate the bunnies' faces, and just the cookies with the frosting were left.

Mom asked her if she had eaten the M&M's first. She said, "Those weren't M&M's. You had her sneaking me my pills."

In Wisconsin, you never know what the weather on Easter will be. My brothers Steve and John, me, and our mom, all dressed up after Easter Sunday services, with bunny balloons.

She had never seen the pastel-colored M&M's and, being in the early stages of dementia, she thought that I was trying to give mom a hand in giving her meds.

The funny thing is, she wrapped what she thought were the pills up in a napkin and put them in her drawer. Even though she did not want to take her pills, she knew that they cost money, so would not throw them away.

I will never be able to make my bunny face cookies without thinking of Grandma.

Easter Lamb

Every Easter for many years, mom's neighbor, Lydia Lempke, would make us one of these lambs and bring it over for Easter. It was a very kind, neighborly thing to do. Now, I make one every Easter for each of our six kids as part of their Easter treat. If you have one of these old lamb cake molds, or even a bunny one, this is a great way to use it. If you don't have one, check the thrift stores. It is a fun tradition to start.

¼ Cup margarine of butter
6 Cups miniature marshmallows
6 Cups krispy rice cereal
cooking spray
3 candies for eyes and nose (I use either M&M's or small jelly beans)
3 dabs of frosting to secure the eyes and nose

The easiest way to make these is in the microwave. In a large microwavable bowl, microwave the butter or margarine and the marshmallows for 2 minutes. Stir to combine. Microwave for 1 minute longer. Stir until smooth.
Add the rice cereal and stir until completely combined.
Spray both halves of the cake mold until covered (1).
Pack the cereal mixture into the face side first, making sure to fill the ears as well. Put the remaining cereal mixture into the back half (2). Place the back half onto the face half and press down to make sure the two halves stick together and to help pack down the face area. Flip onto the back side of the mold. Remove the face side of the cake mold and let set and cool. Once cooled, you can put the eyes and nose on with the dabs of frosting (3). Let dry completely, leaving the back half of the mold on. This takes about 6-8 hours. Once dry and set, you can put the lamb in plastic wrap and tie with a ribbon as a gift (4), or use as part of your buffet or table decor for Easter.

1.

2.
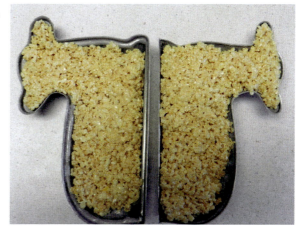

3.

4.

Ham Glaze

This is an easy, tasty glaze/cooking liquid for doing our Easter and Thanksgiving hams. I always cook our ham in one of the large roasting bags. It helps keep it moist and the glaze makes it very flavorful.

Makes enough for a half ham

1 Cup	pineapple juice
⅓ Cup	brown sugar
1½ tsp.	pumpkin pie spice or cinnamon
⅓ Cup	maple syrup

Mix the glaze ingredients in a small bowl

Score ham skin, place cut side down in roasting bag in baking pan. Pour glaze over ham and bake according to directions until done.

That is all that there is to it.

Sometimes we make the ham the day before serving and warm up in pineapple juice in a crock pot. That saves on oven room the day of the holiday.

Hot Mustard (Sweet/Hot)

This wonderful recipe given to me by my cousin Debbie Becker. I was blessed to grow up with a cousin only 6 weeks older than me. Someone at her school, where she worked, gave her a jar of this for Christmas and she was hooked.

*This is a wonderful accompaniment to your Easter ham, and oh, so many other things!
It is also gluten free!*

**1   4-oz. tin of Coleman's Dry Mustard (yes, you will be using the whole thing)
1 Cup   apple cider vinegar
2   large eggs
¾ Cup   sugar
1½ Cups   Hellman's Mayonnaise**

In the top of a double boiler, or medium-sized heavy saucepan, mix the dry mustard and vinegar with a whisk.

Add the eggs and sugar.

Whisk well.

Cook over a low heat, whisking constantly until thickened. This may take a bit; be patient, keep stirring, you don't want it to scorch.

Cool completely.

Whisk the mayonnaise in completely.

Store in a covered container in the refrigerator.

Bring on the hot dogs, pretzels, ham, or anything else that goes with mustard.

My favorite thing to dip into the mustard is pretzels.

This should last for a month or more in the refrigerator, but tastes so good, it probably won't be there that long.

My Deviled Eggs

These are the deviled eggs that my kids like. Nothing fancy, but a good base for whatever you may want to add.

Makes 12

6	hard boiled eggs, peeled and rinsed
½ Cup	Miracle Whip
1½ tsp.	yellow mustard

salt and pepper to taste
paprika for garnish

I have found that the best way to hard boil eggs is to mix about 1 - 2 Tblsp. of baking soda in the pot of water you will be using (depending upon size of pot). I bring the eggs to a boil and then let them simmer for 15 minutes. I run them under cold water and peel them under the running water once they are cool enough to handle. I know there are many methods out there, but this is the one that I prefer. Older eggs peel easier than fresh eggs.

Cut each egg lengthwise into halves. Scoop the yolks out with a small spoon and put in a bowl. Mash with a fork. Add the next 3 ingredients, either spoon or use a small decorator gun to refill the whites with the yolks. Sprinkle with the paprika.

Some people like a little bit of hot sauce in the filling, hence the name "deviled," but my family prefers it without. Feel free to add it if you like.

Leftover Holiday Soup

I make this wonderful soup using many of the leftovers from the holiday. This is a favorite after Easter as well as Thanksgiving.

1 Tblsp. butter or olive oil
1   large onion chopped
1   clove garlic chopped
4 Cups   chicken, turkey, or vegetable stock
2-3 Cups leftover cream or whole kernel corn, or 2 cans
4 Cups   leftover mashed potatoes
2 Cups   leftover cubed ham
salt and pepper to taste
fresh parsley or chives for garnish
Other add-in's: cooked broccoli, carrots, or cauliflower

Heat butter or oil in a Dutch oven. Add onion and cook onion until it softens, add garlic and stir about 30 seconds.

Add the stock, corn, potatoes and ham.

Cover and simmer until heated through and potatoes break up. You can use a potato masher to speed up the process.

Add any additional vegetables. Finish heating.

Salt and pepper to taste.

Carrot Cake Cookies
with Cream Cheese Frosting

A wonderful addition to your Easter dessert selection. A nice soft cookie with lots of flavor. Make it your own. If you don't like coconut or nuts, leave them out. The most important ingredients are the carrots, pineapple, and raisins.

Makes about 4 dozen cookies

3 Cups	all-purpose flour (I make it with gluten free flour and it comes out just fine)
1 tsp.	baking powder
½ tsp.	cinnamon
½ tsp.	baking soda
¼ tsp.	salt
½ Cup	shortening
½ Cup	butter, softened
1 Cup	brown sugar, packed
1 Cup	granulated sugar
2	eggs
1½ tsp.	vanilla extract
1	8-oz. can of crushed pineapple, drained, saving juice
½ Cup	sweetened, flaked coconut, if desired
½ Cup	golden raisins
½ Cup	grated carrot
½ Cup	chopped walnuts, if desired

Frosting:

1	8-oz. package of cream cheese, softened
1 Tblsp.	butter, softened
3 Cups	powdered sugar
1 Tblsp.	reserved pineapple juice

To garnish:
Your choice of
1 Cup toasted coconut
orange edible glitter
chopped walnut pieces or walnut halves

Whisk the flour, baking powder, cinnamon, baking soda and salt together in a bowl.
Beat the butter, shortening, and sugars with an electric mixer in a large bowl until smooth.
Add the eggs and vanilla, mix until well blended.
Mix the flour mixture into the wet ingredients.
Fold in the pineapple, coconut, raisins, carrot, and walnuts.
Preheat oven to 375°.
Drop onto parchment lined baking sheets by heaping teaspoonful, allow about 2 inches between cookies.
Bake until lightly brown and top feels set when touched. About 10-12 minutes, depending on your oven.
Allow to cool on baking sheet about 1 minute before moving to a wire rack. Let cool completely.

To make the frosting:
Beat the cream cheese and butter with an electric mixer until completely smooth.
Add the powdered sugar and pineapple juice and continue mixing until all lumps are out.
You want this to be a nice spreading consistency, so if it is too thin and runny, add a little more powdered sugar.
 If too thick, just a few more drops of pineapple juice at a time, until you have a nice thickness.
Frost cookies once they are cooled, spreading the frosting almost to the edges.
Garnish as desired
To toast coconut: Just put about 1 Cup of coconut in a dry frying pan. Over a low heat, continue stirring until toasted. Watch carefully.

Easter Nests

I don't remember who gave me this recipe originally, but it is one of my favorites.

Makes about 1½ dozen

⅓ Cup sugar
½ Cup creamy peanut butter
½ Cup light corn syrup
1 Cup butterscotch flavored chips
2½ Cups chow mein noodles
2 Cups cornflakes, crushed after measuring
mini malted milk eggs or jelly beans

Combine sugar, peanut butter, corn syrup, and chips in a large microwavable bowl.
Microwave on high in 30-second increments, stirring after each time until chips are melted and mixture is smooth.
This should take about 1½ minutes total, depending upon your microwave.
Stir in noodles and cornflakes, mixing well until everything is coated.
Shape about a ¼ cup scoop onto wax paper, making an indentation for the "eggs" in the middle of each.
Put a few jelly beans or malted milk eggs in the middle of each.
Work quickly, as this mixture sets up quickly.
Let sit until nests set up and dry.
I put each of these into a jumbo muffin-sized paper muffin cup, then into a plastic bag to keep them fresh.

Baby & Bridal Showers

Springtime Cake...46
Rose Cupcakes...47
Party Popcorn Mix...48
Baby Shower Twinkies...49
Baby Face Cupcakes...50
Baby Buggy Deviled Eggs...51
Homemade Butter Mints...52

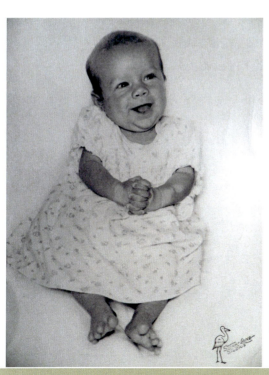

*This is a photo of me as a baby.
See, I was even happy back then!*

Springtime Cake

This is a nice moist cake because of the fillings and frosting.
It needs to be stored in the refrigerator because of the frosting.
You can use your own preserve preference for fillings (for a baby boy shower, you could go with all blueberry, for a baby girl, maybe strawberry). Use your imagination and creativity.

1 white cake mix
water, oil, and egg whites as directed on package

½ Cup	lemon curd (usually located by the jams and jellies)
½ Cup	seedless raspberry preserves
½ Cup	apricot preserves
1	8-oz. tub of frozen whipped topping, defrosted (do not use the lite version in this recipe)
½ Cup	powdered sugar

Bake the white cake mix in 2 round 8 or 9 inch cake pans as directed on package.
Once removed from the pans, let cool completely.
Slice each cake horizontally into 2 rounds, ending up with 4 rounds.
Put one of the top cake rounds, rounded side down on a serving plate.
Spread the lemon curd all over the cake and almost to the edges.
Top with the other half of the same cake, cut side towards the curd, so the flat bottom is on top.
Spread this layer with the raspberry preserves, almost to the edges.
Top this layer with the bottom layer of the second round, cut side up.
Spread this layer with the apricot preserves.
Top with the last round of cake, cut side down, rounded side up.

Mix the defrosted whipped topping in a bowl with the powdered sugar. Make sure lumps of sugar are gone.
This gives it a little more consistency for spreading, and staying on the sides of the cake.
If desired, you could add a drop or 2 of food coloring, for instance, pink or blue for a baby shower, or whatever you like.
Frost the sides of the cake, then the top with the whipped topping mixture.
Be generous with the frosting, this will also cover any cracks in the cake that might have happened transferring the rounds.

I like to decorate mine with gumdrop flowers. Do not use the spice flavored ones. They just don't go well with this cake. I just roll out the gumdrop with a rolling pin on a surface dusted with sugar until it is flat. Then I pinch it in back a little to form a flower and use a small piece of another colored gumdrop for the middle.
I use a green gumdrop cut into wedges and rolled out for the leaves. You can put these on the top right before serving, decorate each slice, or put around the bottom of the cake on the serving plate.
You can use sprinkles, or whatever you like to decorate this cake, but I usually do the gum drop method.

Rose Cupcakes

I found these cute cupcakes years ago and have made them for many occasions, from birthdays to showers.

Makes 12 cupcakes

- 12 mini cupcakes, baked from your choice of cake mix, in mini cupcake liners
- 1 can of vanilla frosting, or homemade
- 6 fruit by the foot rolls, from the fruit snack section of the grocery store, in color of rose desired

mint leaves, or 1 roll green fruit by the foot, or spearmint leaf gumdrop candies

Frost the cupcakes with the vanilla frosting.
Take one roll of the fruit snack and unroll it.
Cut down the middle with a scissors in a wavy pattern the whole length of the snack.
Peel one of the halves off of the wax paper.
Roll up from one end about 4 inches into a tight center of the rose.
Place in the middle of the cupcake with the straight side down, wavy side up.
Loosely wrap the rest of the length around the center section to form the rest of the rose.
Cut leaves out of the green snack, use mint leaves, or cut sections of the spearmint leaf gumdrop and tuck around the rose.

47

Party Popcorn Mix

This is an easy recipe that can be changed up for baby or bridal showers, or even birthday parties, depending upon the colors used.

9-10 Cups popped popcorn (air popped is best, or in a pan with oil, but not microwaved)
½ Cup candy-coated chocolate pieces. Pick colors that work with your party theme.
½ Cup honey roasted peanuts
½ Cup semisweet chocolate chips
1½ tsp. vegetable oil
½ Cup melting chocolate disks of your choice (the kind to make candy with)
1½ tsp. vegetable oil
1 tsp. sea salt
sprinkles, colored sugar, jimmies, or nonpariels, in colors that go with your theme

After popping corn, pick out any kernels that are not fully popped and discard.
Line a large baking sheet with sides with parchment paper or waxed paper.
Spread the popcorn on the baking sheet.
Sprinkle with the candies and nuts.
Melt the chocolate chips and 1½ tsp. oil in the microwave and stir often until smooth.
Drizzle using a butter knife over the popcorn mixture.
Melt the colored chocolate disks with the other 1½ tsp. vegetable oil in the microwave and stir often until smooth.
Drizzle over the popcorn mixture using a butter knife.
Sprinkle with the salt.
Sprinkle lightly with your choice of decorative sprinkles, etc.
Let dry until the melted chocolate drizzles harden.
Break into pieces and store in airtight container or plastic bags.

Baby Shower Twinkies

Sometimes you see a picture and just have to duplicate it. This is one of those. Easy for a no-bake dessert for a shower.

For each baby you will need:

1	Twinkie
2	mini chocolate chips

yellow or white frosting for bonnet (canned or homemade)
pink or blue frosting for arms (canned or homemade)

1	small plastic cake decor pacifier
1	small plastic cake decor bottle
1	6 inch paper doily.

Unwrap the Twinkie.
Place the mini chocolate chips point first into the cake for eyes.
Stick the pacifier into the cake where the mouth would be, you might need to use a knife to make a little hole first.
Pipe white or yellow frosting onto the head in a squiggly pattern for the bonnet.
Pipe pink or blue from the sides up to the middle on each side for the arms. Place bottle in the middle.
Place Twinkie baby on the doily, wrap the sides of the doily upwards, catching some of the arm frosting to hold it on.
Place these side by side on a tray to help the frosting on the doilies set up.
You may need to put something at the end of the row until the end doilies set up with the frosting.

49

Baby Face Cupcakes

A fun, cute recipe that is really more of an idea than a recipe.

1	box cake mix (white or yellow work best for this one)

water, oil, and eggs as directed on package
24	cupcake liners
1	can vanilla frosting
48	chocolate chips
24	inexpensive pacifiers

Bake 24 cupcakes as directed on the package.

Tint the frosting the desired color (pink, blue, or flesh tones; cocoa powder can be used to achieve darker skin tones).

Frost the cupcakes.

Put 2 chocolate chips point down into each cupcake for eyes.

Stick the pacifier into the cupcake where the mouth would be.

Cute as can be, and easy too!

Baby Buggy Deviled Eggs

*This is a fun one that your guests will love!
No need to make a whole tray of them if you don't want to, maybe just place these few on a larger tray of deviled eggs for decoration, or go for it and make them all this way.*

6	hard boiled eggs, peeled, cooled completely, rinsed, and dried with a paper towel
½ Cup	Miracle Whip salad dressing, or similar product
1½ tsp.	yellow mustard
salt and pepper to taste	
32	thin slices of an approximately 1 inch diameter carrot that has been peeled
32	wheel hubcaps: you can use thin slices of a small pickle, ends of small olives, ends of grape tomatoes (for this photo, I just happened to have small pickles on hand, so that is what I used)
16	toothpicks
8	plastic babies (usually found in party or cake decorating stores)

Slice the eggs the long was as you normally would for a deviled egg.

Scoop the yokes into a bowl, mash with a fork, and add the salad dressing, mustard, salt, and pepper.

In 8 of the white halves, stick 2 toothpicks all the way through for the axles.

Thread a piece of carrot onto each of the 4 toothpick ends for the wheels.

Thread your choice of hubcaps onto each of the toothpick ends.

Fill the 8 buggy bottoms with the filling.

Cut each of the 4 egg white halves in half crosswise.

Place each of those halves over the end of the filled buggy for the buggy cover (see picture).

Place a plastic baby on each.

51

Homemade Butter Mints

Sure, you can buy mints. But, once you taste these, the store bought ones just won't do.
These are wonderful on a plate on your shower buffet, or in 2 oz. portion cups at each place setting.
I also have a picture of how I used them as a part of a take home gift at mom's 80th birthday party.
You can do any combination of colors that fit your theme.

Makes about 5-5½ dozen

¼ Cup	butter, softened
⅓ Cup	light corn syrup
1 tsp.	peppermint extract, I prefer this over the plain mint extract for this recipe
3¾ Cup	powdered sugar
1 Cup	granulated sugar

food coloring

In a mixer, combine the butter and corn syrup. Add the peppermint extract, then the powdered sugar, 1 cup at a time, ending with the ¾ cup of powdered sugar.
Separate the "dough" into 3 portions for different colors. For this project, I left one dough portion uncolored. Wrap in plastic wrap.
Add one portion to the mixer and mix in 2 drops of food color. Mix until color is thoroughly blended in. Remove from mixer and wrap in plastic wrap.
Clean the mixer and mixer paddle.
Add the third portion and mix in 2 drops of a different color, Mix until color is thoroughly blended in. Wrap in plastic wrap.
   For a larger project, maybe for wedding favors, I just do a batch in each color that I want to use.
Shape the dough into about ¾ inch balls. Roll each in granulated sugar, then flatten on a wax paper lined baking sheet with a fork to make the lines on top.
Let air dry for at least 24 hours.
Store in a sealed airtight container. No need to refrigerate.

Summer

Summer Fruits...56
Garden Goodies...64
Summer Celebrations...75

Summer Fruits

Raspberry Cream Cheese Muffins...57
Mom's Cherry Cobbler...58
Cherry Pie...59
Banana Raspberry Bread...60
Lemony Raspberry Muffins...61
Belgian Waffles...62
Blueberry French Toast Bake...63

Summer fruits can be enjoyed very simply, like a fruit plate with cottage cheese and a sprinkle of cinnamon (one of my favorites), or in any one of these recipes.

Raspberry Cream Cheese Muffins

A very moist muffin that will have everyone coming back for more.

Makes 24 muffins

4 oz.	cream cheese, light can be used, but not non-fat
½ Cup	butter or margarine, softened
1½ Cups	sugar
2 tsp.	vanilla extract
2	large egg whites
1	large egg
2 Cups	flour
¼ tsp.	baking soda
1 tsp.	baking powder
½ tsp.	salt
½ Cup	buttermilk
2 Cups	fresh or frozen raspberries (if frozen, do not thaw first)

Preheat oven to 350°.

Combine cream cheese and butter or margarine in a large mixing bowl. Beat with mixer until well blended. Add sugar and beat until fluffy. Add vanilla and eggs. Beat well.

Combine flour, baking soda, baking powder and salt. Add flour mixture to cream cheese mixture, then mix in the buttermilk mixing both on low.

Fold in the raspberries.

The foil/paper muffin cup liners are best with this recipe, as they keep the muffins very moist.

Line muffin pans with 24 cup liners. Spoon the batter equally into the liners and bake 25 minutes, or until a wooden toothpick inserted in the center comes out clean.

Remove from pans and cool on a wire rack.

Mom's Cherry Cobbler

This is enough for a 2 quart glass casserole. If using a 9 by 13 inch glass pan, double the recipe.

1¼ Cup	sugar
3 Tblsp.	cornstarch
4 Cups	pitted tart cherries. You can use frozen (defrosted). I prefer the ones that we are lucky enough to get in Door County, WI
¼ tsp.	almond extract
1 Cup	flour
1 Tblsp.	sugar
1½ tsp.	baking powder
½ tsp.	salt
3 Tblsp.	shortening
½ Cup	milk

Preheat oven to 400°.

Blend sugar, cornstarch, cherries, and extract (vanilla may be used if you don't like almond) in a saucepan. Cook stirring constantly until mixture thickens and boils. Pour into ungreased GLASS baking dish (do not use metal, cherries react with the metal).

Keep hot in oven while preparing biscuit topping:

Measure flour, sugar, baking powder, and salt into bowl. Add shortening and milk. Stir until dough forms a ball, scraping sides of bowl to mix well. Drop 6 dollops onto (for a 2 quart baking dish) or 12 dollops (for a 9 by 13 baking dish) onto hot mixture in the dish.

Bake 25-30 minutes or until biscuit topping is golden brown. I recommend putting foil on the oven rack under the rack with the baking dish to catch drips, just in case it bubbles over.

Serve warm with ice cream and/or whipped topping.

Cherry Pie

This is my favorite recipe to make after a trip to Door County to pick up their fantastic cherries.

Makes one 9 inch pie

- 2 unbaked pie crust; purchased, gluten free, or homemade, using pie crust recipe in Basics section (page 189).
- 1⅓ Cups sugar
- ⅓ Cup flour OR ¼ Cup instant tapioca (a great way to make it gluten free)
- 4 Cups washed/pitted red tart cherries (ok to use frozen/thawed) unsweetened, no need to drain the juice from frozen.
- ¼ tsp. almond extract, if desired
- 2 Tblsp. butter or margarine

Preheat oven to 425°.

Roll out 1 crust between 2 pieces of wax paper. Fit into 9 inch pie plate. Patch any holes in the crust to insure that pie filling does not leak through them.

In a bowl, mix sugar, flour or tapioca, cherries and extract if using. Stir well to dissolve most of the sugar.

If using instant tapioca instead of flour to thicken filling, let sit for about 15 minutes to give filling a chance to thicken.

Spoon filling into pie crust.

Dot with the butter.

Roll out the second crust between wax paper and put on top of the pie. Crimp edges with fingers or fork. Trim any excess crust from the sides of the pie plate.

Cut a few slits in the top crust, I like to do it in the shape of a C for cherry, but whatever you like to let steam escape

Put a 3 inch strip of foil around the edges of the pie.

Bake 35-45 minutes, removing foil from edges during the last 15 minutes of baking. Crust should be golden brown and juice from the filling bubbling up just a little through the slits.

If desired, sprinkle with a small amount of sugar and rub with hand onto top crust when you take it out of the oven and while it is still hot.

Banana Raspberry Bread

A wonderful twist that makes banana bread even more moist and tasty.

Makes 2 full-sized loaves or 4 mini loaves

1¾ Cups	flour
1½ Cups	sugar
½ tsp	salt
1 tsp	baking soda
2	large eggs
½ Cup	vegetable oil
1 Cup	mashed ripe bananas
1 tsp.	vanilla
⅓ Cup	water
1 Cup	fresh or frozen raspberries (if using frozen, do not thaw first)
½ Cup	chopped pecans or walnuts, if desired

Preheat oven to 350°.

In a large bowl, combine the flour, sugar, salt, and baking soda. In a separate bowl, combine the eggs, oil, bananas, vanilla, and water.

Stir the wet ingredients into the dry ingredients just until moistened, do not over mix. Fold in the raspberries and nuts, if using.

Pour into 2 greased 8 by 4 inch loaf pans or 4 greased mini loaf pans.

Bake for 55-65 minutes for the regular loaves, or 35-40 minutes for the mini loaves. Use the toothpick test inserted near center of loaf. If it comes out clean, it is done.

Cool for 10 minutes in pan, then using a knife, run along the edges of the loaves, then tip upside down to remove the breads from the pan. Let cool right side up on a wire rack.

These loaves freeze great, just wrap separately in plastic wrap, and then wrap in aluminum foil. Put in a freezer bag.

Lemony Raspberry Muffins

Makes 12

2¼ Cups	all-purpose flour
½ tsp.	baking soda
2 tsp.	baking powder
½ tsp.	salt
1 Cup	sour cream (light is ok, but do not use fat free)
2	large eggs
1 Cup	sugar
½ Cup	vegetable oil
1½ tsp.	vanilla
1 Tblsp.	fresh lemon juice, plus zest of 1 lemon
1 Cup	fresh or frozen raspberries (add to recipe frozen if using frozen)

Preheat oven to 375°

Spray muffin pans.

In a large bowl, combine the flour, baking soda, baking powder, and salt.

In a separate medium bowl, combine the sour cream, eggs, sugar, oil, vanilla, lemon juice, and zest.

Add the wet mixture to the dry, stirring until combined. Do not over mix.

Fold in raspberries.

Divide the batter into the 12 muffin cups and bake 18-23 minutes until toothpick inserted into the muffin comes out clean.

Let cool in pan 10 minutes before removing to a wire cooling rack.

Belgian Waffles

I love making this recipe for the 4th of July. Just top with sugared blueberries, strawberries and raspberries and just a spritz of whipped topping.
 In the fall, you can add a teaspoon of cinnamon or pumpkin pie spice for a great fall treat. One of the best things about this recipe is that you make the batter the night before using. I got this recipe years ago with my waffle iron, and it is the best I have tasted.

Makes about 6 waffles depending on the size of your waffle iron.

2⅔ Cup	all-purpose flour
1 packet	(2¼ tsp.) active dry yeast
2 Tblsp.	sugar
1 tsp.	salt
1¾ Cups	milk
¼ Cup	water
¼ Cup	butter or margarine
3	large eggs

Combine the flour, yeast, sugar and salt in a large bowl. Mix well.

Heat milk, water, and butter or margarine until very warm (120°-130°); butter or margarine do not need to melt.

Add to flour mixture. Add eggs. Using an electric mixer, blend at low speed until moistened. Beat 1 minute at medium speed. Cover bowl with plastic wrap, then foil. Refrigerate overnight.

Preheat your waffle iron according to your manufacturer's directions. Spray with cooking spray.

Put the amount of batter into the iron that your waffle iron normally takes, mine is about ⅔ cup.

Close top of waffle iron and cook until browned, usually once it stops steaming.

Top as desired, or just serve with warm maple syrup.

Blueberry French Toast Bake

A big thank you to my friend Amy Hanten for her original recipe using raspberries. Amy is the host of a TV show named "Living with Amy," which I appear on often. This is a half portion for a smaller family that uses blueberries. Or, you could go half blueberries, half raspberries for a great red, white, and blue look.

- ½ Cup maple syrup
- 5-6 Cups French bread cut into about 1½-2 inch cubes
- 1½ Cups milk
- 3 eggs
- ¼ tsp. cinnamon
- ½ tsp. vanilla
- 1 Cup blueberries
- ¼ Cup brown sugar
- 3 oz. cream cheese, cut into small cubes
- 2 Tblsp. butter

Spray a 9 by 9 baking dish with cooking spray.
Pour the maple syrup into the baking dish, spread evenly.
Add the bread cubes on top of the maple syrup, distribute evenly.
Whisk together the milk, eggs, cinnamon, and vanilla.
Pour the egg mixture over the bread.
Cover with foil, refrigerate overnight.

When ready to bake, Preheat the oven to 350°.
Uncover dish and sprinkle the blueberries over the top.
Add the cream cheese, distributing evenly over the top.
Sprinkle with the brown sugar and dot with the butter.
Cover loosely with foil.
Bake for 50 minutes.
Uncover and bake for another 10-15 minutes until all the liquid is absorbed and top is bubbly.
Let cool a few minutes before cutting into squares and serving.
If desired, serve with additional syrup (maple, raspberry, or blueberry).

My friend Amy Hanten

Garden Goodies

Using what the summer garden gives us: beans, zucchini, and all those tomatoes.

Zucchini Nut Loaf...65
Crispy Zucchini Spears...66
Shrimp with Zucchini and Tomatoes...67
Chicken with Summer Squash...68
Grandma's Cucumber Salad...69
Chocolate Zucchini Cake...70
Cabbage with Italian Sausage...71
Pickled Beets...72
Dilly Beans...73
Pickled Banana Peppers...74

Zucchini Nut Loaf

I have been making this recipe for years, I'm not even sure where I got it originally. It makes two regular-sized loaves or five of the mini loaves, which is what we like to do with just the two of us in the house. Great with a little butter or cream cheese.

3 Cups	all-purpose flour
½ tsp.	nutmeg
½ tsp.	baking powder
2 tsp.	cinnamon
1 tsp.	baking soda
1 tsp.	salt
2 Cups	sugar
2 Cups	shredded zucchini
2	eggs
1 tsp.	vanilla
½ Cup	vegetable oil
½ tsp.	grated lemon peel
1 Cup	chopped walnuts or pecans

Preheat oven to 350°.
In a medium bowl, stir together the flour, nutmeg, baking powder, cinnamon, baking soda, and salt.
In a mixing bowl, beat together the sugar, zucchini, eggs, and vanilla.
Add the oil and lemon peel, mix well.
Stir the flour mixture into the zucchini mixture.
Gently fold in the nuts.
Pour batter into 2 greased regular-sized loaf pans or 5 greased mini loaf pans.
Bake for 55-60 minutes, or 35-40 minutes for mini loaves.
Bread is done when a toothpick inserted near the center comes out clean.
Cool in pan for 10 minutes.
Remove from pan and cool thoroughly on rack.
Wrap and store loaf overnight before slicing.
To freeze, wrap in plastic wrap, foil, then put in a freezer bag.
½ Cup of raisins, dried cranberries, or dried cherries can be added at the same time as the nuts.

Crispy Zucchini Spears

A great side dish for everything from your favorite pasta dish to a bowl of soup.

Makes 2 servings

¾ - 1 lb.	zucchini, small to medium is best (no need to peel)
½ Cup	panko bread crumbs (gluten free can be used)
1 Tblsp.	Parmesan cheese
1 Tblsp.	Italian seasoning
1	large egg

sprinkle of salt
dipping sauce of your choice, Marinara sauce or Ranch dressing are what we like best.

Preheat oven to 450°.
Cut the 2 ends off of the zucchini
Cut in half crosswise.
Cut each half in half lengthwise, then each piece into spears no wider than ½ inch on the edge with the peel.
Beat egg in a shallow pan, even a paper plate with sides will work.
Put the bread crumbs, cheese, and seasoning into a zippered bag.
Line a baking sheet with parchment paper or aluminum foil. Spray with cooking spray.
Dip each piece of zucchini into egg, coating all sides, then drop into the zippered bag.
Once you have about 6-8 pieces in the bag, close bag and shake to coat the pieces well. Place in a single layer on the prepared baking sheet (none touching each other).
Finish coating all of the zucchini, then bake 12-15 minutes until crispy and browned.
Sprinkle with salt.
Serve with dipping sauce of your choice.

Shrimp with Zucchini and Tomatoes

Makes 2-4 servings

1 Tblsp.	olive oil
1	medium uncooked zucchini, cut into ¼ inch slices
1 lb.	uncooked shrimp, large size, peeled and deveined
1 Cup	grape tomatoes, cut in half, or chopped tomatoes
½ tsp.	dried oregano, or Italian seasoning
½ tsp.	salt
¼ tsp.	black pepper
1½ tsp.	minced garlic
¼ Cup	water
1 Cup	cooked spaghetti noodles, I like to use whole grain, but any will do, including gluten free

Heat 2 teaspoons of oil in a large nonstick skillet over medium high heat.

Add zucchini in a single layer; increase heat to high and cook until bottoms are golden, about 2 minutes.

Flip zucchini and cook until golden on other side, about 2 minutes more.

Remove zucchini to a plate with a slotted spoon.

Heat remaining teaspoon of oil in same skillet. Add shrimp; saute 1 to 2 minutes.

Add tomatoes, oregano, salt and pepper; saute until shrimp are almost just cooked through, about 1 minute.

Stir in garlic and water; saute, stirring to loosen bits from bottom of pan, until shrimp are cooked through and tomatoes are softened, about 1 to 2 minutes more.

Return zucchini to skillet; add the cooked pasta and finish cooking until the pasta and zucchini are hot.

Toss and serve.

Chicken with Summer Squash

There's just something about a man that can cook. This is one of the dishes that hubby makes that we both love. It uses some of the treasures from our summer garden, but this dish can be made with frozen squash and canned tomatoes as well.

1 Tblsp.   shortening
2   boneless, skinless chicken breasts cut into 1 inch cubes
2   cloves garlic, minced
¼ tsp.   ground cumin
2 Cups   tomatoes (fresh chopped or canned) with the juice from the tomatoes
3 Cups   cubed yellow summer squash
3 Cups   cubed zucchini squash
salt and pepper to taste

Melt the shortening in a dutch oven, brown the chicken cubes.
After chicken is browned, add the garlic and cumin.
Add the tomatoes, when sauce starts to simmer, add yellow squash and zucchini and cook, covered, on low until squash is tender.
Add salt and pepper to taste.

Wonderful served over rice, or great by itself.

Grandma's Cucumber Salad

Grandma made this several times every summer when Grandpa bought fresh cucumbers from the Farmer's Market

½ Cup   sugar
½ Cup   regular vinegar
½ Cup   canned evaporated milk (Not sweetened condensed milk!)
½   onion sliced thinly
1-2   cucumbers peeled and cut into about ¼ inch slices
          (don't use the really fat cucumbers, the thinner ones are best)
salt and pepper to taste

In a medium-sized bowl, mix the sugar and vinegar together until the sugar is dissolved.
Mix in the canned milk. Add the onion. Add the cucumber slices until there are enough in the bowl that they are no longer covered by the sauce.
Gently stir to get all of the cucumber slices coated. Add salt and pepper to taste.
Refrigerate for at least one hour.
Refrigerate any leftovers.

Chocolate Zucchini Cake

I first tried this moist, delicious cake when my dear friend and neighbor Lin Neuens (pictured with her husband, Randy) baked it for her daughter Nicole's baby shower. She was kind enough to share this recipe with me.
How do you top a cake this full of chocolate taste and moistness?
Might I suggest cherry pie filling and whipped cream, although it is perfect on its own.

3 Cups   flour
1½ tsp.   baking powder
1 tsp.   baking soda
1 tsp.   salt
4   large eggs
3 Cups   sugar
1½ Cups vegetable oil
2 squares unsweetened baking chocolate, melted
   (6 Tblsp. unsweetened baking cocoa and 2 Tblsp. shortening, melted, can be substituted)
3 Cups   shredded zucchini
1 Cup   chopped nuts of your choice, optional

Preheat oven to 350°.
Mix together the flour, baking powder, baking soda, and salt.
Beat the eggs, gradually add the sugar. Add the oil, chocolate, and lastly, the dry ingredients. Stir until moistened, then fold in the zucchini and nuts.
Oil and flour a bundt pan. Pour mixture into bundt pan and bake for about an hour and 15 minutes. Test with a toothpick.
Let cool about 15 minutes in pan. Then put a plate on top of pan, and turn over. It should come out of the pan right away, but if not, leave it there for a couple of minutes and check again.
Once completely cooled, dust with powdered sugar.

Cabbage with Italian Sausage

We live in an area that has acres and acres of cabbage being harvested. We love it, and my hubby makes this wonderful comfort food dish. So simple, yet so tasty.

Makes 4-8 servings, depending on how hungry you are.

1 Tblsp. olive oil
8 oz. Italian sausage, mild or hot
½ large cabbage or 1 small cabbage, cut into bit sized chunks
½ Cup water
salt and pepper to taste
if desired, a sprinkle of red pepper flakes

Brown the sausage in the olive oil in a large covered pan like a dutch oven until fully cooked. No need to drain.
Add the cabbage, give it a good stir, simmer about 5 minutes covered.
Add the water and simmer, covered until the cabbage is tender, stirring every 5 minutes.
Salt and pepper to taste, add the sprinkle of red pepper flakes if you like more spice.

Sounds almost too simple to be tasty, but it is one of our favorites this time of year.
We like to serve it with cheese and crackers.

Pickled Beets

These are wonderful with thinly sliced onions stirred in on the relish tray.

Makes 6-8 pints

10 lbs.	fresh small beets, stems removed
2 Cups	sugar
1 Tblsp.	canning (pickling) salt, DO NOT USE regular table salt
4 Cups	white vinegar

Place beets in a large pot with water to cover. Bring to a boil and let simmer until tender. If beets are a little larger, they can be cut in quarters. Drain, reserving 2 cups of the beet water.
Run the beets under cold water. This will help in the peeling process. Peel the beets.
Put the beets into sterilized pint canning jars
In a large pan, combing the reserved beet water, sugar, canning salt, and vinegar. Bring to a rapid boil.
Pour the hot canning liquid over the beets in the jars until beets are covered. Leave about ¼ inch at top of jar. Put on sterilized lids and seals.
Process in a hot water bath with water fully covering the jars by at least one inch. Process for 10 minutes. If lid does not seal upon complete cooling, just store that jar in the refrigerator as you would pickles.

Pickled beets served with dilly beans; recipe on page 73.

Dilly Beans

These make a wonderful addition to your relish tray.

Makes 4 pint jars

2-3 lbs.	green beans, washed and ends trimmed. Try to use the straightest beans you can find, medium thickness. Don't use older tough beans or too skinny ones. You want to end up with about 4 inch beans once they are trimmed, so they end up fitting nicely in the canning jar.
1 tsp.	cayenne red pepper
4 cloves	garlic
4 heads	fresh dill weed (this is the part that looks like a big snowflake at the end of the stems of leaves)
¼ Cup	canning (pickling) salt, DO NOT USE regular table salt
2½ Cups	water
2½ Cups	white vinegar

Sterilize your canning jars. I found that the easiest way to fill the jars with beans is to place the hot jar on its side, then layer the beans as full as possible. Stand up the jar and you might be able to fit a couple more beans along the inside edges. Add ¼ tsp of the red pepper, a garlic clove, and a head of dill. (If the heads of dill are very large, you can use half of a head.)

Combine the salt, water and vinegar in a pan and bring to a boil. Stir well until the salt is dissolved. Pour the hot liquid into the jars of beans leaving about ¼ inch of room at the top of the jar. Put on sterilized lids and cap seals and process for 10 minutes in boiling water bath which fully covers the jars by at least an inch.

Remove from the hot water bath and let cool. Caps should seal and be tight when pressed in the middle after they are cooled. This process may take a few hours.

If you have one that does not seal, just store it in the refrigerator as you would pickles.

I usually wait at least 2 weeks before eating to let them get fully pickled.

Pickled Banana Peppers

These peppers are a wonderful way to use your excess banana peppers from the garden.
Great on a pizza, sandwich, or relish tray.
Not spicy, just tasty.

Makes 3 pints

1½ lbs.	banana peppers, washed, cut into thin slices, most of the seeds and ribs removed
3 cloves	garlic, peeled
3 Cups	white vinegar
2 Cups	water
2 Tblsp.	Kosher salt
1 Tblsp.	sugar

Fill 3 clean, sterilized canning jars with the sliced peppers, add a whole clove of garlic to each jar.
Heat the vinegar, water, salt, and sugar in a sauce pan, Bring to boiling.
Pour the liquid over the peppers in the jar, they should be totally covered.
Put on the lids and seals.
Let sit until room temperature, then store in refrigerator.
Ready to eat in about 24 hours; give them time to pickle. Should last about 3 months.

Summer Celebrations

A 4ᵗʰ of July Memory...76
The Perfect No-Cook 4th of July Breakfast...77
My Potato Salad...78
Grandma B's Baked Beans...79
Grandma B's German Potato Salad...80
Crispy Cole Slaw...81
Broccoli Salad...82
Asian Cole Slaw...83

A 4th of July Memory

What is your favorite 4th of July memory? Thought I might share mine with you, what it was like in the "old" days, when I was a kid.

There was the parade that anyone could join. We all started at a local school near Sherman Park, the park in Milwaukee we were headed to. We all wore red, white, and blue (if we had it), and everyone who showed up was given a small American flag. We walked the mile or so to the park with our decorated bikes and wagons and flags. There was a school band playing patriotic music.

We were always met at the park by Grandma and Grandpa, aunts and uncles, cousins, and other extended family, who were saving tables and getting the wonderful picnic lunch ready. There were always ham sandwiches, Grandma's homemade baked beans and German potato salad, and watermelon. The park system always provided the cups of ice cream with the wooden spoons when we arrived at the park from the parade. That day was the only day we were allowed to eat dessert first, so the ice cream would not melt.

After a late lunch, there was a judging of all the decorated bikes, wagons, and buggies. The winners won a small toy prize like a Frisbee, or a savings bond.

We never won, but we sure had fun trying.

Families played together in the park, visited, and waited for the fireworks. We went home tired, happy, and full of memories.

I hope that you all get to make some memories with your families this 4th of July weekend.

Happy Birthday America.

The Perfect No-Cook 4th of July Breakfast

one bowl of krispy rice cereal
2 strawberries split down the middle
5 blueberries with the stem end up
milk

This is really not a recipe. It is a memory of something that my Grandma would fix for me if I was at her house during the 4th of July.

You get the snap, crackle, and pop from the cereal, and the red, white, and blue. And, look closely at the picture.

When the blueberry stem fills with milk, most of them take on a star shape.

Fun for the kids, and everyone!

My Potato Salad

4 Cups   peeled potatoes, cut into bite-sized cubes
3   hard boiled eggs, chopped
¼ Cup   chopped onion
1 Cup   Miracle Whip
2 Tblsp.   yellow mustard
salt and pepper to taste
¼ Cup   chopped dill pickle (if desired)
paprika

Cook the potatoes until tender in boiling water, drain, rinse with cold water.
Mix the eggs, onion, salad dressing, and mustard together. Check the seasoning, add salt and pepper to taste.
If desired, add the chopped dill pickle. Fold in the cooled potatoes and mix well.
Garnish with a light sprinkle of paprika if desired.
Refrigerate for at least an hour before eating, refrigerate any leftovers.

Grandma B's Baked Beans

Getting married during the Great Depression, my Grandma B was great at making tasty dishes for just a little bit of money. She served these for the holidays with ham, at summer picnics, or any other time she was cooking for a crowd, usually with her German potato salad and crispy cole slaw. Grandpa's prize was the onion that she baked in the middle; that was his. She usually doubled this recipe, but even this feeds a crowd.

- 1 lb. dry navy beans, picked over and washed
- 1 tsp. baking soda
- 2 Cups warm water
- 1½ tsp. salt
- ½ tsp. dry mustard
- ½ Cup brown sugar
- ½ Cup molasses
- 1 medium onion, skin removed, left whole
- several slices of bacon

Preheat oven to 350°.

Look over beans, removing any debris or stones. Rinse beans, drain, and put in a large kettle.

Add water to cover plus about 2 inches more.

Add the baking soda.

Bring up to a boil, turn down the heat and simmer on low for 30 minutes.

Drain in a colander and rinse.

Place beans in a large baking dish.

Mix the water, salt, dry mustard, brown sugar, and molasses. Pour over the beans.

Place the whole onion in the center of the beans.

If necessary, add a little more water so that beans are all covered.

Place several strips of bacon over the top of the beans for flavor, or leave them out if you want a vegan dish.

Put a cover on the baking dish, or cover with foil.

Bake for 3 to 4 hours, checking every hour to see if more water is needed to cover beans.

At the 3-hour mark, check if beans are the softness that you like by tasting one.

Bake until desired softness is achieved.

The bacon on top will not get crispy. If you like, finish it up in a frying pan, cut in pieces and add to the beans.

79

Grandma B's German Potato Salad

Grandma made this potato salad for so many of our family get togethers, whether it be a picnic in summer, or alongside the Easter ham. Just the smell of it makes me think of her.

1 qt.	cooked, peeled potatoes, sliced
1	medium-sized onion, cut in half and sliced thinly
¼ lb.	bacon, cut in small pieces
½ tsp.	salt
¼ tsp.	pepper
½ Cup	sugar
½ Cup	white vinegar
½ Cup	water
1 Tblsp.	cornstarch
4	hard cooked eggs, sliced

a sprinkle of paprika for garnish

Put potatoes and onions in a bowl.
Cook bacon until crispy.
Remove bacon from pan, add to potato mixture, and drizzle ¼ cup bacon fat over potatoes and onions.
Add salt and pepper.
In a small saucepan, mix the sugar, vinegar, water, and cornstarch together.
Heat on low, stirring constantly until thick and glossy.
Pour over potato mixture, stir together.
Garnish with hard cooked eggs, and paprika, if desired.
Best served warm.

Crispy Cole Slaw

One of my greatest pleasures in the kitchen, is making a recipe written in my grandma's handwriting and serving it in one of her serving dishes.

This recipe is one that my grandma made for Easter, 4th of July, and Christmas. I remember she jazzed it up at Christmastime by adding pomegranate seeds on top.
This is a great dish for a dish to pass, as it does not contain mayonnaise.

1	large head cabbage
1	carrot
1	small onion
1	green pepper
2	stalks celery
1 Cup	white vinegar
1 Cup	sugar
½ Cup	vegetable oil

salt and pepper to taste

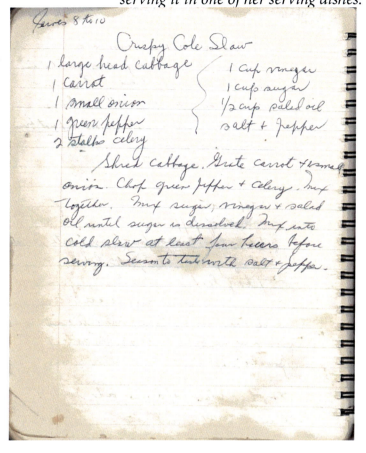

Shred the cabbage. Grate the carrot and onion.
Finely chop the green pepper and celery.
Mix the vegetables together in a large bowl.
Mix the sugar, vinegar, and salad oil until sugar is dissolved.
Stir the sauce into the vegetables and mix well. Add salt and pepper to taste.
Refrigerate for at least 4 hours before serving.

81

Broccoli Salad

A special thank you to my mom's best friend, Miyako Mukai, for sharing this recipe with me years ago.
It has become a family favorite.

1   large bunch of broccoli cut into flowerettes
1   small red onion, chopped
about ¼ head cauliflower cut into flowerettes
about 6 slices bacon cut up and cooked until crispy
about ½ Cup shredded cheddar cheese.

Combine the above ingredients with:
1 Cup   Miracle Whip
½ Cup   sugar
2 Tblsp. white vinegar

Toss well with salad ingredients and refrigerate at least one hour.
Other ingredients that you can add, if you like, are golden raisins and sliced almonds.

Asian Cole Slaw

My cousin's wife, Becky Hoffman Marquardt, made this wonderful salad for my aunt Phyllis's 80th birthday party. She was kind enough to share the recipe. This makes a huge batch for a large gathering, but can be cut in half. I suggest making this shortly before serving. You can prep the crunchy stuff, the vegetables, and dressing separately the day before and combine before serving. The Ramen noodles don't stay crunchy for a second day, but it still tastes just fine, and you probably won't have leftovers.

2	14-oz. packages of shredded coleslaw cabbage, or 1 bunch of chopped Napa cabbage (I like the shredded package as it also usually contains carrots, which add a little extra color)
5	green onions, thinly sliced (whites and greens)
½ Cup	butter or margarine
3	packages of Ramen noodles, just the cheap brick type packages, doesn't matter what flavor, you won't be using the flavor packets
½ Cup	sunflower seeds (without the shells)
2 oz.	sliced almonds

Dressing:

⅔ Cup	vegetable oil
2 Tblsp.	soy sauce
1 Cup	sugar
½ Cup	apple cider vinegar

My cousin Scott and his wife Becky Hoffman Marquardt, with their children Lucas and Mallory.

Mix the cabbage and onions together in a large bowl.

Melt the butter or margarine in a very large skillet or dutch oven.

Crush the Ramen noodles into much smaller pieces, separating chunks.

Brown the noodles, sunflower seeds and almonds by adding them to the melted butter or margarine, cooking on low and stirring very frequently.

After browning, let cool on paper towel to absorb some of the excess butter or margarine.

If not using until later, store the cooled crunchy mixture in an airtight container.

Mix together the dressing. I prefer doing this in a mason jar with a top, or any other container that can be shaken. The sugar needs to be dissolved before using the dressing.

If mixing the dressing the night before, you might need to mix in the sugar that has settled at the bottom of the jar before using.

15 minutes before serving:

Pour the dressing over the vegetables, mix together well. Let sit for about 10 minutes.

Drain out the extra dressing (I did this by using a slotted spoon to put the salad into the serving dish that I was using).

Mix the dressed cabbage with the crunchy mixture.

Fall

Apples...86
Pumpkins...94
Soups...103
Pasta...112
Football Season...119
Halloween...125
Thanksgiving...130

Apples

Apple Pie...87
Apple Raspberry Crisp...88
Crockpot Apple Butter...89
Grandma's Apple Slab Cake...90
Apple Cinnamon Smoothie...92
Caramel Apple Bread Pudding...93

Apple pie, page 87

Apple Pie

When I met my husband, I found out how much he loves all things apple, so I happily perfected my apple pie to his taste. Since he has become gluten free, I had to tweak it just a little more. If you like your apple pie with a little texture to the apples, use fresh. My hubby prefers that all of the apples in a pie are soft, and so do I. To accomplish this, I use frozen, thawed apples and do not drain the juice after defrosting. This probably goes against all the pastry chefs out there who only like using fresh apples, but this is what works best for us.

Pie crust for two 9 inch crusts (purchased, my basic recipe for regular or gluten free on page 189, or your favorite pie crust recipe)
- 6 Cups apples; peeled, cored, and sliced
- 2 Tblsp. butter
- ¾ Cup sugar
- ¼ Cup flour OR for gluten free, 2 Tblsp. instant tapioca
- ½ tsp. cinnamon
- a sprinkle of nutmeg
- a dash of salt

Peheat oven to 425°.

Roll out half of the dough between 2 sheets of wax paper. Peel off one of the sheets, turn it into the pie plate and press with fingers to seal any holes in the crust.

Mix the sugar, thickener (flour or tapioca), cinnamon, nutmeg and salt with the apples in a large bowl. If using the instant tapioca to make it gluten free, let it thicken in the bowl for 15 minutes. Pour the apple mixture into the pie crust. Dot with the butter.

Roll out the second crust between wax paper and put in the pie. Crimp the edges with fingers or fork to seal. Cut off any extra crust with a knife. Cut slits in the top crust.

Cut several 3 inch strips of aluminum foil and put around the edges of the pie to avoid excessive browning.

Use an oven with 2 racks, on the bottom rack, place a piece of aluminum foil with the edges turned up a bit to catch drips. You will be happy you did this if the pie bubbles over.

Bake for 40-55 minutes, or until crust is golden brown and juice bubbles through slits on top crust. Remove foil covering from the edges for the last 15 minutes or so of baking.

While baking, mix:
- ½ Cup sugar
- 1 tsp. ground cinnamon

Right after pulling pie out of oven, place pie plate on a cooling rack, then rub a tablespoon or so of the cinnamon sugar onto the top crust.

Save the extra cinnamon sugar for the next time you bake an apple pie, or it is wonderful sprinkled on buttered toast. I grew up on homemade cinnamon toast.

If you have extra pie crust that you have cut off the edges of the pie before baking, make a memory with a child, or just yourself.

Roll out the dough and either sprinkle with cinnamon sugar, or spread with your favorite jam and bake until golden along with the pie on a small baking sheet or foil. This will not take nearly as long to bake as the pie, so keep an eye on it. One of my favorite childhood memories was being allowed to roll out my own little "pie" with my grandma.

Apple Raspberry Crisp

Growing both apples and raspberries, we love this combination of flavors.

Makes 12 servings

8 Cups	apples, peeled and thinly sliced (we prefer the tart ones, but use whatever you like)
2 Cups	fresh raspberries (unsweetened frozen can be used, but do not thaw)
1½ Cups	packed brown sugar
1 Cup	all-purpose flour (gluten free can be used)
1 Cup	oats
¼ tsp.	ground nutmeg
2 tsp.	ground cinnamon
⅔ Cup	margarine or butter, softened

Preheat oven to 375°.
Grease 9 by 13 inch pan. Spread apples in the pan, top with the raspberries.
Mix the brown sugar, flour, oats, nutmeg, cinnamon and margarine or butter well. Sprinkle over apples.
Bake for 30-40 minutes until apples are soft and topping is golden brown.
Serve while warm.

I love to serve this with cinnamon ice cream, but vanilla works great too!

You can also cut this recipe in half and bake in an 8 by 8 pan for the same amount of time.

Crockpot Apple Butter

*We have a number of apple trees on our little farm, so we mix a variety into our apple butter.
Use whatever kind you like best.*

20 Cups   apples, peeled, cored, and sliced (actually, you can fill the crockpot with even more, whatever fits in a 5 quart crockpot, fill it to the top)
1½ Cups   sugar, use a little more if doing tart apples, a little less if you are using really sweet apples
1½ tsp.   cinnamon
¼ tsp.   cloves
¼ tsp.   salt

Fill up the crockpot as much as possible with apples.
Mix the sugar, spices and salt in a small bowl and pour over apples.
Put the cover on and cook on low all day or overnight. Stir.
Use an immersion blender to get nice and smooth.
Cook down a little more until desired consistency.
I can these for 10 minutes in sterile ½ pint jars. The quantity that you end up with depends upon how much the apples cook down.

Grandma's Apple Slab Cake (also known as Frosted Apple Pie Slices)

This was the favorite dessert that my grandma made. Honestly, I think it is one of the reasons that my hubby married me. Now that he is gluten free, I do a gluten free version. The changes are in the recipe. The dough can be tricky to work with, but the recipe is well worth the effort.

Crust:

3 Cups	all-purpose flour (gluten free can be used)
½ tsp.	salt
3 Tblsp.	granulated sugar
1 tsp.	baking powder
1 Cup	margarine (2 sticks) softened
2	egg yokes
½ Cup	very cold water

Filling:

8 Cups	apples, thinly sliced, peeled, pared (you can use frozen, just thaw first, no need to drain the liquid)
1½ Cups	sugar
½ tsp.	cinnamon
½ Cup	flour (or for gluten free, ¼ Cup instant tapioca)
2 Tblsp.	butter or margarine

Frosting:

1½ Cups	powdered sugar
	pinch of salt
1 tsp	softened butter or margarine
½ tsp.	vanilla
4 tsp.	warm water

Preheat oven to 350°.

Mix the crust ingredients with a mixer, or in a bowl with a spoon until ingredients are thoroughly blended. Form into a ball and wrap with plastic wrap.

If dough is very sticky, refrigerate until it is more workable. You will need a 15 by 10 inch jelly roll pan.

Divide the dough in quarters. I have found that the easiest way to work this dough is to take 2 pieces of wax paper and spray each with cooking spray. I lay one sprayed piece with the sprayed side up, place ¼ of the dough on top, then top the dough with the sprayed side of the other piece of wax paper.

Using a rolling pin, roll out to fit approximately ½ of the bottom and sides of the jelly roll pan. Take off the top piece of wax paper and use the bottom piece to put the dough into half of the pan.

Do the same with another of the quarter pieces of dough. At this point, you can use your fingers to press the dough all over the bottom and sides of the pan making sure there are no holes in the bottom crust that the juice from the filling can get through.

To make the filling:

Put the apples, sugar, cinnamon, and flour (or tapioca) in a large bowl. Stir well. If using the tapioca, let set for 15 minutes in the bowl and stir again.

Spoon the filling into the bottom crust, spreading as evenly as possible. Dot with the 2 Tblsp. of butter.

Make the top crust in the same half and half manner as the bottom crust. Cover as much of the filling as possible, trying to seal the edges to avoid leaking during baking.

Line the bottom rack of your oven with aluminum foil to save yourself some clean up if this bubbles over.

Bake for 1 hour. It will be golden brown and the filling will be bubbling out of any slit in the top of the crust.

Let cool completely.

To make the frosting:

Mix frosting ingredients until thoroughly mixed. If too thick, add just a little bit more warm water. Frost the entire top of the slab apple cake with a thin layer of the frosting, which is more like a glaze.

Let set and cut into desired-sized squares.

This may seem like quite the process, but the end product is so worth it!

Apple Cinnamon Smoothie

Having an abundance of apples in our orchard, it is always nice to have a nice healthy recipe to use some of them.
One can only eat so much apple pie, or so I am told.

Makes 2 servings

1 Cup	crushed or cubed ice
1	banana, peeled and cut in chunks
1	apple, peeled, cored, and thinly sliced. Save 2 thin slices with peel on for garnish if you like.
⅓ Cup	apple juice
½ Cup	plain Greek yogurt
1 tsp.	vanilla
1 tsp.	ground cinnamon
1 Tblsp.	sugar, or your favorite sweetener to taste, if desired

Whipped cream to garnish, if desired

Place all ingredients into blender in order shown, blend until smooth.
Pour into 2 glasses.
Garnish with whipped cream, a little sprinkle of additional cinnamon, and apple slice, if desired.

Caramel Apple Bread Pudding

This wonderful comfort food will not only make your house smell great, but tastes yummy! This makes a smaller batch, so if you are feeding more than 4, just double the recipe and make in a 9 by 13 inch pan.

Makes 4 servings

2 Cups	older white bread, cut in cubes (I use gluten free bread)
1 Tblsp.	butter or margarine
2	apples, peeled, cored, and cut into small cubes
¼ Cup	sugar
1 tsp.	cinnamon
½ Cup	raisins, regular or golden
2 Cups	milk
2	eggs
1 tsp.	vanilla

caramel ice cream topping
whipped cream

Preheat oven to 350°.

Spray a 9 by 9 inch baking pan with cooking spray.

Put the cubed bread in the pan.

Melt the butter or margarine in a small pan.

Saute the apples on low until soft, stirring often.

Spread the apples over the bread cubes.

Mix the sugar and cinnamon together.

Sprinkle the sugar and cinnamon mixture over the bread and apples.

Sprinkle the raisins evenly over the top.

Mix the milk, eggs, and vanilla together in a bowl with a whisk. Pour over the bread mixture.

Let sit for about 30 minutes to let the bread absorb as much of the liquid as possible.

Bake for 35-40 minutes.

Top should be golden brown when done.

Serve warm, drizzle with caramel ice cream topping and garnished with whipped cream.

Store any leftovers covered in refrigerator.

Pumpkins

Pumpkin Chipotle Pasta Sauce...95
Pumpkin Zucchini Cranberry Bread...96
Roasted Pumpkin Seeds...97
Turtle Pumpkin Pie...98
Pumpkin Tiramisu...99
Pumpkin Torte...100
Pumpkin Cake Roll...101
Pumpkin Butter...102

Pumpkin Chipotle Pasta Sauce

This sauce is wonderful over your favorite pasta, or my Butternut Squash Ravioli.

Makes about 4 servings

1 Tblsp.	butter
¼ Cup	chopped onion (white or yellow)
1 clove	garlic, minced
1 Cup	pumpkin puree
1 Cup	chicken or vegetable stock
¾ tsp.	ground chipotle powder
1 tsp.	ground sage
¼ tsp.	pumpkin pie spice
¾ tsp.	salt
⅓ Cup	milk

Melt the butter in a medium saucepan.
Cook the onion and garlic on low about 3 minutes.
Whisk in the other ingredients.
Bring to a boil, then simmer for about 10 minutes, covered.
Serve tossed with your favorite pasta.

Pumpkin Zucchini Cranberry Bread

Makes 2 full-sized loaves or 5 mini loaves

3 Cups	flour
1 tsp.	baking soda
½ tsp.	baking powder
½ tsp.	salt
1½ tsp.	pumpkin pie spice
3	large eggs, lightly beaten
2 Cups	sugar
1 Cup	canned pumpkin
1 Cup	margarine or butter, melted
1 Tblsp.	vanilla extract
1 Cup	shredded zucchini
1 Cup	chopped walnuts or pecans
½ Cup	sweetened dried cranberries (if desired)

Preheat oven to 350°.
Combine the dry ingredients in a medium-sized bowl.
Combine eggs and sugar. Add pumpkin, melted margarine or butter, and vanilla. Mix well.
Mix egg mixture into dry ingredients until combined well, do not over mix.
Stir in zucchini, nuts, and dried cranberries.
Pour into 2 greased regular-sized loaf pans or 5 mini loaf pans.
Bake for 45-50 minutes for regular-sized pans, 30-40 minutes for mini pans. Use toothpick test to check if done.
Cool in pans about 10 minutes, then remove to wire rack to cool completely.

Wrap each loaf individually in plastic wrap once cooled.
Can be frozen, just put the wrapped loaf into a freezer bag.

Roasted Pumpkin Seeds

My kids love roasted pumpkin seeds.
These disappear whenever I make them.
I usually do a batch of salted and a batch with Cajun seasoning.
You might find a seasoning that you want to experiment with.
When I serve them with Halloween treats, I label them Witches' Warts.

2 Cups   Fresh pumpkin seeds, washed and drained
2 Tblsp.   Melted butter
salt, Cajun seasoning, or garlic salt (whatever seasoning you would like to use)

Preheat oven to 325°.
Line a jelly roll pan with foil.
Spray with cooking spray.
Toss the seeds with the butter and spread on the pan in a single layer.
Bake, stirring several times until seeds are dry and toasted, you might have to test a few.
This should take about 20-30 minutes, depending upon your oven.
Sprinkle with salt or seasoning of your choice.
Let cool on a piece of paper towel. This will also soak up any excess butter.
Store in an airtight container.

Turtle Pumpkin Pie

This recipe combines another two of my favorites, pumpkin anything and turtle anything.

Makes 6-8 servings

1	graham cracker pie crust
¼ Cup	caramel ice cream topping
½ Cup	pecan pieces
1 Cup	milk
2	packages (4 servings each) vanilla-flavored instant pudding
1 Cup	canned pumpkin
1½ tsp.	pumpkin pie spice
8 oz.	frozen whipped topping, thawed

additional caramel topping, pecans, and chocolate syrup for decorating

Spread the caramel topping evenly in the bottom of the graham cracker crust.

Sprinkle with the pecan pieces.

Beat the milk, pudding, pumpkin, and spice with a whisk in a medium-sized bowl until combined.

Stir in 1½ cups of the whipped topping until well blended.

Spread over the prepared crust.

Hint* I always find it best to put a graham cracker crust that is in a foil pan on top of another firmer plate to keep from breaking when moving, as well as easier cutting, as I always tend to cut through the foil pan.

Refrigerate at least 2 hours.

Top with the remaining whipped topping.

Garnish with additional caramel topping, pecans, and a drizzle of chocolate syrup, if desired.

Pumpkin Tiramisu

This dessert combines two of my favorite desserts: Pumpkin anything, and tiramisu.

¾ Cup	canned pumpkin
1½ tsp.	pumpkin pie spice
¼ tsp.	salt
¼ Cup	sugar
½ Cup	whipping cream
4 oz.	mascarpone cheese, softened
1 Tblsp.	powdered sugar
½ Cup	whipping cream
1	3-oz. package of ladyfinger cookies, about 12
¼ Cup	maple syrup
pumpkin pie spice	

Line a standard-size bread pan with plastic wrap, making sure to have a piece going crosswise that is longer, so you can pick up cake with the ends. Set aside.

In a bowl, combine pumpkin, pumpkin pie spice, and salt.

In a mixing bowl, combine ½ Cup whipping cream and sugar.

Beat with electric mixer on medium until soft peaks form.

Fold into pumpkin mixture until thoroughly mixed in.

In another bowl, combine the mascarpone cheese and powdered sugar until no lumps are left.

Gradually beat in the last ½ cup of whipping cream until mixture is thickened, do not overbeat.

Layer 6 ladyfingers in the prepared pan, crosswise.

Drizzle with 2 Tblsp. of the maple syrup.

Top with half of the pumpkin mixture.

Level off with a spoon.

Layer the last 6 ladyfingers on top of the pumpkin filling, crosswise, like the first 6.

Drizzle with the remaining 2 Tblsp. of maple syrup.

Top with the remaining pumpkin mixture, level off.

Top with the mascarpone cheese mixture, smoothing with a spoon.

Cover. Refrigerate for 12-24 hours.

Tiramasu can be lifted out of the pan using the plastic wrap.

Sprinkle the top with a little pumpkin pie spice using a sifter (I found that an old mesh tea strainer works great for this).

I find it easier to slice and make nice serving pieces if frozen, then sliced while partially frozen.

Cut in 6 slices to serve.

Pumpkin Torte

My Grandma B knew that I loved pumpkin anything.
When she made this one, it always put a smile on my face.
There is an option of doubling the cheesecake layer to make a thicker layer.

Crust:
2 Cups	graham cracker crumbs
1 stick	butter or margarine, melted
½ Cup	sugar

Cheesecake layer (this layer can be doubled, if desired):
8 oz.	cream cheese, softened
¾ Cup	sugar
2	eggs

Pumpkin Layer:
2 Cups	canned pumpkin
3	egg yokes (save the whites, you will be using those later)
½ Cup	sugar
½ Cup	milk
½ tsp.	salt
1 tsp.	cinnamon
¼ Cup	cold water
1	envelope gelatin, unflavored
3	egg whites, or pasteurized egg whites equivalent to 3 egg whites
¼ Cup	sugar

Preheat oven to 350°.
Mix the crust ingredients together.
Press evenly into the bottom of a 9 by 13 baking dish.
Put the cream cheese and sugar into a large bowl.
Mix with a mixer until all the lumps are gone. Mix in the eggs.
Pour over the prepared crust and spread out evenly with a spoon.
Bake for 20 minutes (if you double the cheesecake layer, bake for 30-35 minutes).
Let cool completely.
Meanwhile, in a saucepan, mix the pumpkin, egg yokes, sugar, milk, salt, and cinnamon.
Cook in the saucepan under low/medium heat until mixture thickens (5-7 minutes).
Mix the cold water and unflavored gelatin until well blended.
Add to the hot pumpkin mixture and stir well.
Pour hot pumpkin mixture into a large bowl to cool completely.
Once the cheesecake layer and pumpkin mixture are cooled, beat the 3 egg whites, adding the ¼ cup of sugar gradually until stiff peaks form.
Fold well into the cooled pumpkin mixture.
Pour the pumpkin/egg white mixture over the cooled cream cheese layer.
Spread evenly.
Refrigerate for at least 4 hours before slicing into squares.
Serve with whipped topping.

Pumpkin Cake Roll

Makes about 12 slices

3	large eggs
¾ Cup	sugar
⅔ Cup	pumpkin
½ tsp.	vanilla extract
¾ Cup	all-purpose flour
1 Tblsp.	pumpkin pie spice
1 tsp.	baking powder
½ tsp.	salt
1 Tblsp.	powdered sugar
6 oz.	cream cheese, softened, cut into cubes
1 tsp.	butter or margarine
1 Cup	powdered sugar
½ tsp.	vanilla extract

Preheat oven to 375°.

Line a 15 by 10 by 1 inch jelly roll pan with waxed paper. Spray with cooking spray.

In a large bowl, beat the eggs for about 3 minutes. Gradually add sugar, then beat for 2 minutes, or until mixture becomes thick and lemon colored. Beat in pumpkin and vanilla.

Combine flour, pumpkin pie spice, baking powder, and salt in a separate bowl; fold into pumpkin mixture. Spread batter evenly into prepared pan.

Bake for 10-15 minutes or until cake springs back when lightly touched, being careful not to overbake. Cool for 5 minutes.

Turn pan upside down onto a linen kitchen towel dusted with 1 Tblsp. of powdered sugar. Peel off waxed paper. Roll up cake in the towel, starting with one of the short sides. Cool completely, seam-side down.

To make filling: In a small bowl, mix cream cheese, margarine or butter, the cup of powdered sugar, and vanilla until light and fluffy.

Unroll cooled cake: Spread filling evenly over cake until about ½ inch from the edges. Roll up again, putting the end seam at the bottom. Cover and refrigerate for at least 1 hour before serving. I serve this with a little whipped cream that I added a sprinkle of cinnamon to.

Pumpkin Butter

Not only does pumpkin butter taste amazing, but it makes your house smell like fall at the same time.

12 Cups	pumpkin from pie pumpkins, peeled, seeds and inside membrane removed, cut into cubes about 2 inches.
1 Cup	apple cider
1 Cup	water
½ Cup	maple syrup
½ Cup	brown sugar
1 Tblsp.	pumpkin pie spice

Combine all ingredients in a crockpot and cover. Cook on low until pumpkin softens.
Using an immersion blender, blend until all chunks disappear.
Cook down until you get a nice spreading consistency.
The cooking can be done overnight, if desired.
I put these in sterile canning jars that can also be used in the freezer, and freeze them. It is hard to can pumpkin butter safely using home methods.
I usually make 4-oz. jars. Makes approximately 3 cups, depending upon how long you cook it down.

Soups

Potato Sausage Soup...104
Wild Rice Mushroom Soup...105
Beefy Tomato Mushroom Soup...106
Calico Bean Soup...107
Curried Carrot Soup...108
Butternut Squash Soup...109
Minestrone Soup...110
Pumpkin, Barley, and Sage Soup...111

Potato Sausage Soup

Makes 4-6 servings

1 Tblsp.	olive oil
1 lb.	Italian sausage, mild or hot, depending on how you like it
½ Cup	chopped onion
5	cloves garlic, finely chopped
1 Tblsp.	dried Italian seasoning
4	medium potatoes, peeled, thinly sliced and cut in quarters
4 Cups	chicken broth
2 Cups	milk
½ tsp.	salt, approx.
3 Cups	chopped kale or spinach

Heat oil in a large soup pot. Cook sausage until no longer pink, crumble with a spoon as it cooks.

Add the onion, garlic, Italian seasoning and cook for about 5 minutes until the onion and garlic soften.

Add potatoes, broth and milk. Cook about 30 minutes until potatoes are very soft. Taste for saltiness and add salt as needed.

I like to take a potato masher and mash some of the potatoes, this helps them release more starch and makes the broth a little thicker

Add the kale or spinach and cook an additional 15 minutes, or until kale is tender. Spinach cooks much quicker.

Wild Rice Mushroom Soup

This is one of my favorite soups to make with my leftover turkey and turkey stock after Thanksgiving, but can be made with chicken and chicken stock as well.

2 Tblsp.	olive oil
½ Cup	chopped onion (white or yellow)
½ Cup	chopped celery
8 oz.	sliced white mushrooms
2 Cups	frozen mixed vegetables (carrots, peas, corn, green beans)
½ tsp.	salt
3 Cups	leftover cubed turkey or chicken
6 Cups	turkey or chicken stock
1½ Cups	cooked wild rice
¼ tsp.	ground pepper
½ tsp.	poultry seasoning

In a large pot, saute the onion, celery, and mushrooms in the olive oil until they are softened but not too brown. Add the remaining ingredients and heat to simmer.

Simmer for about 30 minutes.

Taste test to see if additional salt is needed.

Beefy Tomato Mushroom Soup

This soup sounds too simple to taste so good, but trust me, it is delicious.

Makes about 8 servings and freezes well

6 Tblsp.	butter or margarine
1 lb.	fresh mushrooms (button or baby bella), cleaned and sliced
1 Cup	onion, yellow or white, chopped
1 Cup	celery, chopped
1 Cup	carrots, chopped
2	garlic cloves, chopped
3 Tblsp.	all-purpose flour
	or for gluten free, ¼ cup cold water + 1½ Tblsp. cornstarch mixed together
8 Cups	beef broth
1	15-oz. can of tomato sauce
2 Cups	tomatoes, peeled and chopped (or 1 pt. jar of home canned)
½ tsp.	ground pepper
1 tsp.	salt

fresh parsley and sour cream to garnish

In a large kettle melt the butter or margarine.
Add the mushrooms, onion, celery and carrots. Saute until tender, add the garlic and stir for about 30 seconds.
Add the flour or water/cornstarch mixture. Stir until well blended.
Add broth, tomato sauce, tomatoes, salt and pepper. Cover and cook about 30 minutes.

Calico Bean Soup

This is a very inexpensive, hearty soup, especially if you saved the bone from your last ham. You need to soak the beans the night before, but it is worth the effort.

This soup makes at least 8 servings and freezes well

1	20-oz. bag of dried 15-bean mix
8 Cups	water for soaking the beans
1 Cup	onion, chopped
1 Cup	green or red pepper (or a combo of both), chopped
1	ham bone with attached leftover ham if possible
1 piece	cheesecloth large enough to enclose the ham bone, butcher's string to tie
8 Cups	water
1	14.5-oz. can of diced tomatoes or 1 pt. of home canned
1½ tsp.	chili powder
2	cloves of garlic, chopped

juice from 1 lemon

Rinse the beans in a colander after checking for any stones or other non-bean pieces. Put in a large soup pot and add 8 cups water. Let soak covered overnight.

The next day, drain the water from the beans and add the beans back to the pot. Add the onion, peppers, and water.

Put the ham bone in the middle of the piece of cheesecloth and either tie diagonal corner to diagonal corner, repeating with the other 2 corners, or tie with butchers string. (This helps keep the grizzly parts that might be on the ham bone out of the soup.)

Add the enclosed ham bone to the pot.

Cook on low for 2 hours, stirring occasionally.

Add tomatoes, chili powder, lemon, and garlic.

Simmer an additional 30 minutes.

If the bean mixture came with a flavor packet like ham or Cajun, feel free to add it at this point. Otherwise, just salt and pepper to taste.

Take out the cheesecloth with the ham bone inside Let cool, remove any ham still on the bone, chop, and add to the soup.

Curried Carrot Soup

Makes about 4 servings and freezes well

1 Tblsp.	olive oil
½	onion, chopped
1 lb.	carrots, chopped
2 Cups	vegetable or chicken broth
1 Cup	water
½ to 1 tsp.	sweet curry powder
salt to taste	

To garnish:
  toasted coconut
  Greek yogurt
  chives, if desired
  chive flowers, if desired

Heat oil in a large pot. Saute onion over medium heat until onion is softened.
Add the carrots, broth, water, and curry powder.
Simmer about 20 minutes until carrots are very soft.

Meanwhile, if garnishing with coconut, in a dry pan on low heat, toast about ½ cup coconut until golden brown, stirring often.
Once the carrots are soft, use an immersion blender right in the pot and puree, or wait until very cool and puree in a blender.
Salt to taste. Add more curry powder, if desired, after tasting.
Garnish with a sprinkle of the coconut, a dollop of plain Greek yogurt, chives, and a chive flower.

Butternut Squash Soup

This is a wonderfully easy to make soup with minimal ingredients, but big taste.

Serves 6

1	butternut squash (about 3 lbs., which should yield about 4 cups of squash), peeled and seeded
2 Tblsp.	olive oil
1	medium onion, chopped
6 Cups	vegetable stock or chicken stock

salt and pepper to taste
a dash of nutmeg
sour cream to garnish, if desired
chopped green onions to garnish, if desired

Cut the squash into about 1-inch pieces. In a large soup pot, heat the oil.
Add onion and cook until softened. Add the squash and stock.
Bring to a simmer and cook until squash is tender.
Using an immersion blender, blend until pureed, or let cool and puree in blender.
If soup is too thick, just thin with a little stock or water.
Add salt and pepper to taste and just a dash of nutmeg.
Garnish with sour cream and/or green onions, if desired.

Minestrone Soup

This recipe makes a nice big pot of soup and freezes well.

2 Tblsp.	olive oil
1 Cup	onions (white or yellow), chopped
1 Cup	mushrooms, sliced, if desired
1 Cup	carrots, peeled and sliced
1	stalk of celery, chopped
3 cloves	garlic, minced
4 Cups	tomatoes (fresh, peeled and chopped; or canned)
1 tsp.	salt
6 Cups	water
1 Tblsp.	Italian seasoning
1 Cup	grated zucchini
1	14.5-oz. can green beans
1	15-oz. can garbanzo beans, drained and rinsed
1	15.5-oz. can kidney beans drained and rinsed
2 Cups	spaghetti sauce
½ Cup	green pepper, chopped
1 Cup	uncooked medium shell pasta
8 oz.	Italian sausage links or bulk Italian sausage, if desired

salt and pepper to taste
Parmesan cheese for garnish, if desired

In a large soup pot or Dutch oven, heat the olive oil over a medium heat.
Add the onions, mushrooms, carrots and celery.
Cook, stirring often, until vegetables start to soften, about 5 minutes.
Add the garlic and cook, stirring constantly for about 30 seconds.
Add the tomatoes, salt, water, and Italian seasoning.
Cook until carrots are softened.
Add the zucchini, green beans, garbanzo and kidney beans, green pepper, and spaghetti sauce.
Heat until bubbling.
Add the shell pasta and cook until pasta is desired consistency.
If you are looking at a vegetarian dish, stop at this point.
If not, slice the sausage links and brown the slices, or bulk sausage, in a separate pan until cooked thoroughly.
Drain off the fat from the meat.
Add the cooked sausage to the soup.
Garnish with the Parmesan cheese after serving.

Pumpkin, Barley, and Sage Soup

After my mom and I had this soup out, I had to find a recipe to make this at home. A perfect fall soup that is easy to make. This is my own take on it:

Makes 4 servings

2 tsp.	olive or vegetable oil
1	small onion, chopped
1 Tblsp.	fresh sage leaves, chopped
½ Cup	quick cooking barley
4 Cups	vegetable or chicken stock
1¾ Cup	pumpkin (a 15-oz. can)
2 Tblsp.	maple syrup

salt and pepper to taste
more chopped sage to garnish, if desired

In a large pot or Dutch oven, heat the oil.
Add the onion and fresh sage. Cook for about 3 minutes, stirring often.
Add barley and broth.
Bring to a boil, reduce heat, simmer covered for 12 minutes. Stir occasionally.
Stir in pumpkin and maple syrup. Heat through.
Add salt and pepper to taste.

Pasta

Enjoy Those Fresh Tomatoes! Pasta...113
Butternut Squash Mac & Cheese...114
Butternut Squash Ravioli...115
Pasta with Italian Sausage and Vegetable Sauce...116
Italian Pasta Bake...117
Mary's Pasta Salad...118

Enjoy Those Fresh Tomatoes! Pasta

We always have fresh tomatoes in the garden in the summer and this is one of our favorite ways to use them. This dish is easy to double or more for additional servings.

For 2 servings

- ¼ Cup olive oil
- ¼ Cup chopped onions
- 4 oz. brie cheese
- 1-1¼ Cup chopped fresh tomatoes
- 2 cloves garlic, minced or 1 large clove garlic, minced
- 6-8 oz. bulk Italian sausage, or 2 Links
- ¼ Cup shredded fresh basil
- 4 oz. dry spaghetti pasta or linguine pasta, regular, whole grain, or gluten free

salt and pepper to taste

While the brie is cold, remove as much of the rind as possible, if you don't like the rind. Cut the Brie into pea-sized pieces.

Using a nice-sized pasta bowl or large mixing bowl, put the oil, onions, cheese, tomatoes, and garlic in the bowl. Give it a stir to coat all and just a light sprinkle of salt to get the tomato juices flowing. Let sit in bowl for 30-45 minutes. This allows the flavors to meld together and the cheese to soften.

If using sausage links, you can either remove the sausage from the skin, or cut in slices.

In a sauce pan, cook the sausage until thoroughly cooked through and browned. Drain the fat.

Cook the pasta as directed on the package.

Add the hot, drained pasta, cooked sausage, and fresh basil to the bowl with the tomato/brie mixture. Toss. Salt and pepper to taste.

If you want the dish a little warmer, you can microwave the whole bowl for a minute or so, just to heat things up and melt the brie just a little more.

Butternut Squash Mac & Cheese

A wonderful combination of squash, sage, and the classic mac and cheese, with less cheese required.
This recipe can be done using gluten free pasta.
The stock can be vegetable stock to make it vegetarian.

Makes 4 large servings

3 Cups	uncooked, cubed butternut squash, or 1 12-oz. package of frozen butternut squash
1½ Cups	uncooked penne pasta, or similar pasta
½ Cup	chicken or vegetable stock
½ Cup	milk
½ Cup	shredded cheddar cheese
2 Tblsp.	butter or margarine
1 Tblsp.	fresh sage leaves, chopped
¼ tsp.	salt
⅛ tsp.	pepper, freshly ground if possible
½ Cup	shredded cheddar cheese for on top

additional chopped fresh sage for garnish, if desired

Preheat oven to 350°. Spray 9 by 9 baking pan with cooking spray.
If using frozen squash, cook according to package directions.
If using fresh squash, put in a saucepan, cover with water, cover, and simmer until soft.
Cook pasta as directed on package, cooking the minimum cooking time on the package.
Once squash is cooked, put in a medium saucepan.
If using fresh squash, remove from the pan it is cooking in with a slotted spoon and put in the medium saucepan without the cooking liquid.
Add the stock, milk, cheese, and butter to the pan containing the squash.
Cook on low until cheese and butter are melted, stirring constantly and mashing the squash a little while cooking.
Add the sage, salt, and pepper. Stir well, then add the cooked pasta and mix well.
Pour into prepared pan.
Top with the last ½ cup of cheese.
Bake for 20 minutes until it starts to brown and cheese on top is melted.
Garnish with additional sage if desired.
This recipe can be doubled and baked in a 9 by 13 pan for 20-25 minutes.

Butternut Squash Ravioli

This ravioli is a wonderful fall dish just as is, or paired with the Pumpkin Chipotle Pasta Sauce in the Pumpkin Section, page 95.

6 - 8 servings

1 Cup	mashed, cooked butternut squash
½ tsp.	ground black pepper
½ tsp.	salt
⅓ Cup	grated Parmesan cheese
1	egg yoke
½ Cup	mascarpone cheese
1	16-oz. pkg. round or square wonton wrappers
2 Tblsp.	butter

chopped sage leaves and grated Parmesan cheese for garnish

Place first 6 ingredients in a bowl and mix well.
Fill a small bowl or ramekin with water.
On a work surface, place one wonton wrapper down.
Dip finger in water and moisten the outer edges of the wonton wrapper with water (about ¼ inch in from all sides).
Place about 1 measuring teaspoon of filling in the center.
Fold in half and press around the edges to seal, making sure to seal well.
Place on a tray lined with plastic wrap.
Fill the remaining wonton wrappers.
If necessary to create a second or third layer on the tray, put plastic wrap between layers, this helps keep them from sticking together.
In a Dutch oven or larger saucepan, bring about 4 inches of salted water to a boil.
In a large frying pan, melt the 2 Tblsp. butter
Drop about 6 of the ravioli at a time into the boiling water.
Cook for about 2 minutes until the ravioli float to the top.
Remove with a slotted spoon to the frying pan with the butter and fry for about a minute on each side.
Transfer to a serving plate. Garnish with the sage and Parmesan cheese, if desired.

Pasta with Italian Sausage and Vegetable Sauce

I love to serve this with cooked fresh green beans from the garden, tossed with a little olive oil and garlic powder.
To make this recipe gluten free, use gluten free pasta and sausage.

Makes 4-6 Servings

8 oz.	penne pasta (can substitute gluten free pasta)
4 Cups	combination of peeled 1-inch cubed eggplant, peeled zucchini cut into 1-inch cubes, yellow summer squash cut into 1-inch cubes (if you don't have one of these, or don't like one, just leave that kind out, as long as you have 4 cups total)
½ Cup	chopped onion
1 Tblsp.	olive oil
1 tsp.	minced garlic
8 oz.	mild Italian sausage (can substitute gluten free Italian sausage)
2 Cups	chopped fresh tomatoes (including juices) or canned tomatoes (including juices), or tomato puree
1½ tsp.	Italian seasoning.
3 tsp.	grated Parmesan cheese

salt and pepper to taste

Preheat oven to 425°.
Cook pasta according to package directions.
Combine the 4 cups vegetables, onion, olive oil and garlic.
Line a baking pan with sides with foil, spray with cooking spray, spread the vegetable mixture onto the tray.
Bake for 20-30 minutes or until tender.
In a large skillet, cook Italian sausage until no longer pink, drain off fat. Stir in tomatoes and seasoning.
Add the roasted vegetables and simmer for about 5 minutes. Toss with the drained pasta.
Season with salt and pepper to taste. Sprinkle with Parmesan cheese and fresh basil to garnish, if desired.

Italian Pasta Bake

*One of our favorites. Can be made with gluten free pasta if desired.
Any tubular-shaped pasta like penne can be used.*

Makes 4-6 servings

2 Tblsp.	olive oil
4 oz.	sliced mushrooms
1	red or green pepper, chopped
½	medium onion, chopped
3-4	links of Italian sausage, or 6-8 oz bulk Italian sausage (we look for brands that are gluten free)
6 oz	tubular pasta, like penne, or whatever your favorite might be
1	30-32-oz. jar or can of your favorite red pasta sauce
4-5 oz.	shredded mozzarella, cheese

Fresh basil to garnish, if desired

Preheat oven to 375°.
In a large saute pan, heat the olive oil.
Saute the mushrooms, pepper, and onion as well as the sausage links cut into slices or bulk sausage.
When the sausage is cooked, set vegetable and sausage mixture aside.
Cook the pasta in salted boiling water until it is almost done.
Drain the pasta.
Add the pasta back to the pot it was boiled in.
Add the vegetable and sausage mixture as well as the red pasta sauce.
Stir together.
Grease a 9 by 9 inch baking pan.
Pour the pasta mixture into the pan.
Cover with foil.
Bake for about 30 minutes until everything is heated.
Add the cheese on top and bake uncovered an additional 10-15 minutes until cheese is bubbly and melted.
Garnish with fresh basil, if desired.

Mary's Pasta Salad

This recipe is from my friend and neighbor Pat Fredricks. When I asked her for a recipe to share, she immediately thought of her sister-in-law Mary's pasta recipe.

¼ Cup	water
½ Cup	sugar
4 Cups	rotini pasta (spirals), cooked, drained, rinsed in cold water (we did this one with gluten free pasta and it worked fine)
6	hard cooked eggs, sliced or chopped (I chopped 4 to stir in and sliced 2 to garnish)
½ Cup	shredded carrots
1 tsp.	dried minced onion
½ Cup	chopped celery
2 Cups	salad dressing (the sweet version of mayonnaise)

In a small saucepan, boil the water and sugar for about 1 minute.
Let cool.
Mix together the pasta, eggs, carrots, minced onion, and chopped celery.
Mix in the salad dressing.
Add cooled sugar water and mix in.
If desired, save some of the sliced eggs for garnish.
Chill.

Football Season

Cheesy Football...120
Chili...121
Meatballs in Football (Snap)py Sauce...122
Krispie Football Field...123
Cinnamon Orange Snack Mix...124

*Hubby and myself at Lambeau Field, home of the team we cheer for ~
The Green Bay Packers*

Cheesy Football

We live in Wisconsin, that means that football and cheese go hand in hand.

1	8-oz. package of shredded cheese (your choice of cheddar, taco blend, marble jack)
2	8-oz. packages of cream cheese, softened
½ Cup	salad dressing from a jar, the sweeter kind, not mayonnaise
½ Cup	grated Parmesan cheese
¼ tsp.	ground black pepper
3	green onions, chopped
½ Cup	ground pecans or ¾ Cup real bacon bits
1	slice of cheese (yellow, white, or orange)

Mix the shredded cheese, cream cheese, salad dressing, Parmesan cheese, and pepper with a mixer or in a food processor until well blended.

Stir in the green onions.

Wrap in plastic wrap and refrigerate for about 2 hours.

Form cheese mixture into a football shape on a plate.

Press the ground pecans or bacon bits all over the sides and top of the football.

Cut the slice of cheese into 1 long slice and several smaller slices to make the laces on the top of the football.

Chili

A not-too-spicy version that we always start making once the football season starts. Great for a crowd.

Makes 8-12 servings

1 Tblsp.	olive oil
1	large onion chopped
1	46-oz. can of tomato juice
8 Cups	canned tomatoes, or chopped fresh with skins removed. I usually use 2 quarts of my home-canned tomatoes, including the juices
2	15-oz. cans of kidney or black beans, or 1 of each
1 Tblsp.	chili powder
1 tsp.	salt
1	green pepper, chopped
1½ lbs.	ground beef, browned and cooked, drained
6-8 oz.	elbow macaroni, cooked and drained (gluten free can be used)

In a large kettle, cook the onion in the olive oil until slightly softened. Add the tomato juice and tomatoes, beans, chili powder, and salt. Simmer for 1 hour.

Add the green pepper and cooked hamburger. Simmer for an additional hour. If it is too thick, it can be thinned with a little water.

Add the macaroni right before serving so it does not get mushy. Stir well.

Serve with your favorite chili toppings (chopped onion, grated cheese, sour cream, jalapeno slices, and chopped avocado are a few of ours).

We always put out a bottle of Tabasco sauce, just for the guests who like it more spicy.

Meatballs in Football (Snap)py Sauce

This is a great crockpot dish for during the football season, or any time that you would like a great, hot appetizer.

2 lbs. ground beef
¾ Cup canned evaporated milk
1 envelope onion soup mix
1½ tsp. Worcestershire sauce

Football (Snap)py Sauce:
2 Cups ketchup
1 Cup brown sugar
1 Tblsp. Worcestershire sauce

If baking the meatballs, preheat oven to 350°.
Mix together the ground beef, milk, onion soup mix, and Worcestershire sauce.
Form about 1½ inch meatballs.
Brown meatballs in a pan, turning often until cooked through, or bake on a sheet pan with sides, lined with foil, until cooked through.
Take out of fat and place on paper towels. Pat with additional paper towels to remove excess fat.

Make the Sauce:
Mix the ketchup, brown sugar, and Worcestershire sauce in a crockpot.
Stir until well blended and heat.
Once sauce is hot, add meatballs. Keep on low in crockpot.

Krispie Football Field

A fun dessert for your football party, no baking required.

4 Tblsp.   butter or margarine
4 Cups   miniature marshmallows
6 Cups   krisp rice cereal
1   can vanilla frosting
green food coloring
11 candies (Hershey Kisses or other smaller chocolate)
11 candies (another shape of chocolate) I used Hershey Kisses and Rolo candies
If desired, plastic football and goal posts from cake decor store

In a large microwave-safe bowl, put the butter or margarine and marshmallows.
Microwave for 2 minutes. Stir.
Microwave for another minute. Stir well.
Add the krisp rice cereal and mix well.
Spray a 9 by 13 inch baking pan.
Pat the mixture into the pan evenly (I use a sandwich bag sprayed with cooking spray on my hand to make this job easier).
Let this layer cool completely.
Remove about ¼ of the frosting from the can, leave this part white.
Tint the remaining ¾ of the can green using the food color.
Spread green frosting evenly over the football field.
Put the white frosting in a decorator gun.
Draw a 50 yard line down the middle, and draw the 2 end zones.
Add another line between the 50 yard line and the end zones on each side.
If desired, write 50 on both sides of the field at the middle line.
Put your plastic football on the 50 yard line.
Line up 11 players per team on each side of the 50 yard line (you could use the same candy in 2 different colored wrappers and just leave them in the wrappers for the 2 teams if you like, otherwise with 2 different shapes, I unwrap them).
Add your goal posts, if using, and you have an awesome dessert, as well as decoration for your football snack table.

123

Cinnamon Orange Snack Mix

A wonderful sweet snack mix that will disappear quickly once you put it out for your guests.

1	12-oz. can mixed nuts or peanuts (I used honey roasted peanuts with this batch and they were great)
1	7.5-oz. package Bugles corn snacks
2	egg whites
3 Tblsp.	orange juice
1⅓ Cups	sugar
2 tsp.	cinnamon
1 Cup	dried cherries or cranberries (I used the orange flavored ones to bump up the orange flavor)
1 Cup	chow mein noodles

Heat oven to 275°.
Line a jelly roll pan with foil and spray with cooking spray.
Mix the nuts and Bugles in a large bowl.
Mix the egg whites, orange juice, sugar, and cinnamon in a bowl until well mixed with a whisk.
Pour the egg white mixture over the Bugle mixture.
Stir until well mixed and coated completely.
Pour mixture onto the prepared jelly roll pan and spread out evenly.
Bake for 35 minutes, stirring every 10 minutes.
Add the dried fruit and chow mein noodles.
Mix well and bake for an additional 10-15 minutes until light brown and crispy.
Cool completely, then store in an airtight container.

Halloween

Blood, Worm, and Eyeball Soup...126
Monster Mash with Fingers...127
Ghosts & Monster Smiles...128
Halloween Deviled Eggs...129
Orange Jack-O-Lantern Cookies...129

I have always loved Halloween! Dressing up, having fun with your friends, and of course, the treats!

125

Blood, Worm, and Eyeball Soup

A fun one for the kids, using simple ingredients. Super simple.

1	family size can of condensed tomato soup (23.2-oz. or so)
8 oz.	spinach flavored (green) spaghetti noodles, broken into about 4-inch lengths, cooked as directed on package
1 lb.	batch of my Italian meatballs (page 172), or Football meatballs (without the sauce, page 122), or 1 bag of frozen meatballs
¼ Cup	fresh basil, shredded, if desired

salt and pepper to taste

Cook the meatballs, whichever style you are using.
Make sure they are cooked completely and drained of excess fat.
Make the tomato soup as directed on can, using water, not milk (to keep the bloody color).
Add the basil, if using.
Salt and pepper to taste.

There are two ways of serving:
Add the pasta to a single serving bowl, add a few meatball "eyeballs."
Add the soup to almost cover.
Or:
In a crockpot:
Add the prepared soup, pasta, and meatballs.
Scoop out servings into bowls with a soup ladle.

I kind of like doing the individual bowl serving, it shows off the look of the worms, etc.

Monster Mash with Fingers

This is another fun one for Halloween. Serve with witches' hats (triangular-shaped tortilla chips; even better if you can find black and orange ones during the season).

Monster Mash
3   ripe avocados
⅓ Cup   tomato, chopped
½   small onion, chopped
salt and pepper to taste

Fingers
5   longer baby carrots
1 Tblsp. or so of cream cheese
1 or 2   red radishes

Cut avocados in half, remove seed from each. Use a spoon to remove the "meat" from each.
Mash with a potato masher or fork. It can be a little chunky.
Stir in the tomato and onion.
Add salt and pepper to taste. Put into an appropriate-sized bowl.
Cut a wedge off of the end of each carrot, as shown on picture.
Put a little cream cheese in that wedge.
Cut radishes to make fingernails.
Stick a fingernail onto the end of each carrot finger, letting the cream cheese hold in place.
Stick the fingers into the dip, so they resemble a hand coming out.

Ghosts & Monster Smiles

Sometimes you find something while searching the internet that is just too easy and cute not to share, this is one of those things.

For the Ghosts:
½   banana
2   chocolate chips

Just poke the chocolate chips, pointy side first into the half banana for eyes.
Don't make too far ahead of time or they will turn color on you.

For Monster Smiles:
a red apple cut into slices, leaving on the red skin
lemon-lime soda.
peanut butter
miniature marshmallows

Soak the apple in the soda for about 10 minutes to help prevent browning.
Pat the apple slices dry with a paper towel.
Spread on some peanut butter and stick the marshmallows in between two slices for teeth.

Halloween Deviled Eggs

1 completed recipe of My Deviled Eggs (See Page 40)
12 black olives

Slice each black olive in half the long way. Cut ½ of the olive into legs for the spider. Place the legs on the deviled egg, place the other half of the black olive, cut side down on top of the legs. You don't have to do all of the eggs on the platter this way, just a few accent ones are fine, or, do them all if you like.

Orange Jack-O-Lantern Cookies

1 completed recipe of Orange Sugar Cookies (See Page 198)

Use a pumpkin cookie cutter to make the shape, and with a toothpick or tip of a knife draw the jack-o-lantern faces onto the cookies.

129

Thanksgiving

Recipe for Laughter...131
Candied Sweet Potatoes...132
Crescent Rolls...133
Green Fluffy Stuff...134
Wild Rice and Cranberry Bread...13
Stuffing Waffles...136

Recipe for Laughter

Thanksgiving time, 1990 something. I collect and display pilgrim and turkey statues in my home during that time of year. I had a pilgrim pair that I set on the back of the um, commode in my downstairs guest bath. I went into the bathroom one night and the pair was facing the wall, instead of facing the room, so I turned them around the way that they had been. The next day, they were facing the wall again. The only one home was my hubby, so I asked him if he had turned them around. His reply was, "Yes, I cannot go to the bathroom with them watching."

Ok, so we had a little laugh and I moved them to another location. Well, he was leaving on a business trip for a few days, so while he was gone, I made them a couple of blindfolds out of red ribbon and placed them where they had been originally. He came home that night, went to use the bathroom, and I heard this roar of laughter. He said, "Now I have a couple of hostages in the bathroom!"
We laughed until we cried.

Candied Sweet Potatoes

I make these for both Easter and Thanksgiving.

3 Tblsp. butter or margarine
⅓ Cup brown sugar
⅓ Cup maple syrup
½ tsp. pumpkin pie spice or cinnamon
1 40-oz. can of yams or sweet potatoes in light syrup, drained
1 Cup miniature marshmallows

Preheat oven to 350°.

Melt Butter or margarine in a large skillet. Add brown sugar, maple syrup, and spice. On medium heat, cook until sugar is dissolved and mixture starts to bubble.

Lower heat to low. Add sweet potatoes or yams and continue cooking, stirring often until coated and mixture starts to thicken.

Transfer to a greased 8 X 8 or 9 X 9 pan. Bake for about 20 minutes or until bubbly.

Add the marshmallows, sprinkle on top and continue baking for about 5 minutes until melty.

Crescent Rolls

*I make these for both Easter and Thanksgiving.
Yes, you can buy the kind in the can, but these are worth the extra effort.*

Makes 32 rolls

2	pkgs. active dry yeast
¾ Cup	warm water (105°-115°)
½ Cup	sugar
1 tsp.	salt
2	large eggs
¼ Cup	shortening
¼ Cup	softened margarine
4 Cups	all-purpose flour

additional butter or margarine

Preheat oven to 400°.

In a large bowl, dissolve yeast in the warm water, stirring with a wooden spoon until dissolved.

Mix in the sugar and let sit for about 15 minutes, stirring well.

Add the salt, eggs, shortening, margarine, and 2 cups of the flour, mixing by hand until as smooth as possible.

Stir in remaining 2 cups of flour and mix until smooth.

Form into a ball, leave in bowl and cover. Let rise in a warm place until about double in size.

If your room is not as warm as you would like, I have had great success putting a heating pad on low, putting a dish towel on top of it, then placing the covered bowl on top of the dish towel. It takes about 1½ hours for the dough to double in size.

Divide the dough in half. Roll each half into about a 12-inch circle (I usually do this on parchment paper to avoid sticking).

Spread the circle lightly with softened butter or margarine. Using a pizza cutter, cut the circle into 16 equal wedges. I cut the circle into 4 wedges, cut each of those in half once, then again.

Line a baking pan with parchment paper. Starting at the wide end of each piece of dough, begin rolling towards the point.

Tuck the point underneath, and place the roll on the parchment about an inch apart (you may need to use 2 pans).

Repeat with the remaining dough. Cover loosely with plastic wrap and let sit in a warm spot until double in size (about 1 hour).

Bake 12-15 minutes or until golden brown.

Brush each roll with melted butter once they are out of the oven.

I have made these the day before, then reheated in the oven, covered, and then brushed with butter right after taking them out of the oven.

Green Fluffy Stuff

I make this salad for both Easter and Thanksgiving. It is a modified version of a popular recipe changed to accommodate my family's tastes, as some don't like nuts and some don't like coconut.

1	4-serving package of instant pistachio pudding mix (we use the sugar-free)
1	20-oz. can crushed pineapple, drained (save the juice)
2 Cups	miniature marshmallows
1	12-oz. container of frozen whipped topping, thawed (we use the light, but not the fat free)
½ Cup	maraschino cherries, drained and chopped

In a large bowl, combine the pudding and pineapple, as well as about ¼ cup of the drained pineapple juice. Mix until pudding no longer looks dry.

Add the marshmallows and whipped topping, fold together until fully mixed.

Fold in the cherries. Refrigerate for at least an hour. Can be made a day ahead.

Serve in a pretty bowl, or individual servings.

If desired, you could add ½ cup flaked coconut and/or ⅓ cup chopped pecans or walnuts.

Wild Rice and Cranberry Bread

One of my favorite breads to make the day after Thanksgiving to make fabulous sandwiches out of that leftover turkey, or to enjoy with a hot bowl of soup. Time to haul out that bread maker that has been collecting dust. This recipe is worth the effort.

- 1¼ Cups room temperature water
- ¼ Cup skim milk powder
- 1¼ tsp. celery salt
- 2 Tblsp. honey
- 1 Tblsp. olive oil
- 3 Cups bread flour, or all-purpose flour
- ¾ Cup cooked wild rice (I use the soup grade to save money, but if you want to use the good stuff, feel free)
- ⅛ tsp. ground black pepper
- 1 tsp. bread machine yeast
- ⅔ Cup dried cranberries, regular or orange flavor

Add all of the ingredients into the bread machine in the order shown. Select basic cycle and start the machine. That is all there is to it.

Stuffing Waffles

You might even want to make extra stuffing just so you can have these for breakfast the next day. Think of crunchy pockets of goodness to catch the yoke of an egg. Savory and delicious.

**Enough leftover stuffing to fill ½ or a full waffle iron, depending upon how hungry you are
1 or 2 poached, over easy, or sunny side up eggs; whatever your preference**

Spray the waffle iron thoroughly with cooking spray after it is preheated.
Fill the waffle iron with however much stuffing you would like, close the top of the waffle iron, and push down to help make the waffle indentations.
Cook until heated and crispy. Transfer to a plate and top with your favorite eggs.

Delish!

Winter

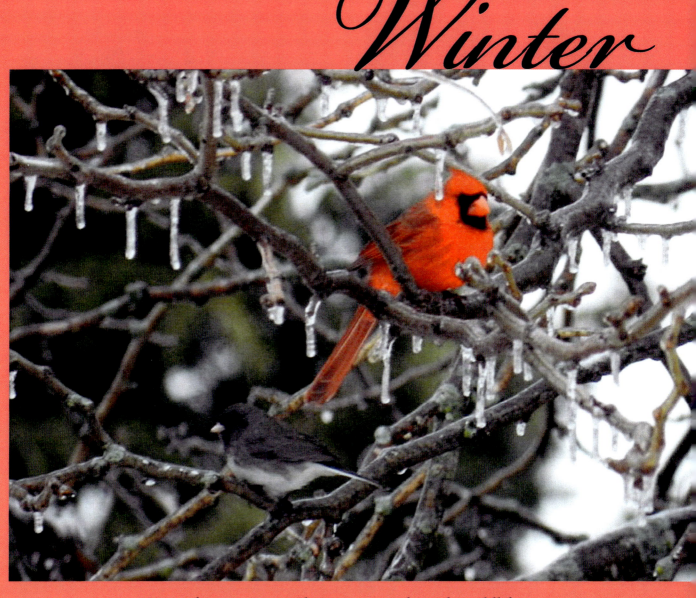

Winter for me means Christmas, watching the wildlife out of our windows and staying warm with comfort food.

Christmas Cookies & Desserts...140
Christmas Gifts & Candy...149

Christmas Cookies & Desserts

Grandma's Gingerbread Folks...141
Three Ribbon Cookies...142
Snickerdoodles...143
Almond Thumbprints...144
Cranberry-Orange Biscotti...145
Eggnog Crème Brûlée...146
Graham Cracker Torte...147
Sweet Potato Pie...148

Me holding a tray of Christmas cookies, from an article written about me in our local women's magazine.

Grandma's Gingerbread Folks

Whenever you bake these during the holidays, your house will smell amazing.

1 Cup   shortening
1 Cup   sugar
1 Cup   dark molasses
½ Cup   water
5 Cups   all-purpose flour
¼ tsp.   allspice
½ tsp.   nutmeg
1½ tsp.   ground ginger
1 tsp.   baking soda
1½ tsp.   salt

candies and frosting for decorating. I use the vanilla frosting that I use on my sugar cookies (see page 203).

Cream shortening and sugar. Blend in molasses and water.

Whisk together flour and other dry ingredients.

Add the dry ingredients to the shortening mixture and mix on low until well blended.

Wrap dough in plastic wrap and refrigerate for 3 hours to overnight.

Preheat oven to 375°.

Roll dough about ¼ inch thick on lightly floured surface. Cut out with gingerbread people shaped cutters.

Bake on ungreased or parchment lined pan for 10-12 minutes or until dough looks set. Do not over-bake.

Remove from pan and place on cooling rack.

Once completely cooled, decorate with icing and candies of choice.

I put my icing in a small decorator gun to get the piping done, then put dots of frosting to hold mini chocolate baking pieces for eyes and buttons.

Amount that this recipe makes is dependent on the size of the cutters used.

Three Ribbon Cookies

This is one of the many Christmas cookies that my mom would make every year as gifts, we all love them.

Makes about 6 dozen

2 Cups	margarine or butter, softened
2 Cups	sugar
2	eggs, beaten
1 tsp.	vanilla
4½ Cups	all-purpose flour
2½ tsp.	baking powder
¾ tsp.	salt
1 Cup	candied red cherries, chopped (the ones like they use in fruitcake)
2 oz.	unsweetened baking chocolate, melted
½ Cup	chopped walnuts
3 Tblsp.	poppy seeds

Preheat oven to 350°.
Cream butter or margarine, add sugar, eggs, and vanilla. Beat until well mixed.
Add flour, baking powder, and salt. Mix well.
Divide dough into 3 equal parts.
To one part add the chopped cherries, mix well.
To one part add the chocolate and nuts, mix well.
To one part add the poppy seeds, mix well.
Line standard bread pan with plastic wrap or wax paper.
Pat the chocolate dough evenly into the bottom of the pan.
Pat the poppy seed dough evenly on top of that.
Pat the cherry dough evenly on top.
Cover and refrigerate overnight.
Lift the dough out of the pan using the paper or wrap that you lined the pan with.
Cut dough the long way into 3 pieces.
Slice each of the long pieces thinly and put onto parchment lined cookie sheet, leaving about 1½ inches in between slices.
Bake for 10-15 minutes until very lightly brown.
Cool on rack.

Snickerdoodles

This recipe makes a lot of cookies relatively inexpensively, with the added bonus of making the house smell great!

Makes 5-6 dozen

- 3 Tblsp. green granulated sugar
- 3 Tblsp. red granulated sugar
- 4 tsp. ground cinnamon
- 1½ Cups sugar
- ½ Cup shortening
- ½ Cup butter or margarine, softened
- 2 eggs
- 2¾ Cups all-purpose flour
- 2 tsp. cream of tartar
- 1 tsp. baking soda
- ¼ tsp. salt

In a small bowl mix the green sugar with 2 tsp. cinnamon.
In another small bowl, mix the red sugar with 2 tsp. cinnamon.
Preheat oven to 400°.
In a large bowl, beat sugar, shortening, butter or margarine, and eggs until well blended.
Stir in flour, cream of tartar, baking soda, and salt until mixed well.
Shape dough into ¾-1 inch balls. Roll into one of the colored sugar mixtures until well coated. Place about 2 inches apart on a baking sheet lined with parchment, or an ungreased cookie sheet.
Bake 8-10 minutes until centers are set. Cool about 1 minute, then remove from baking sheet to cooling rack.

Almond Thumbprints

Very tasty and light cookies.

Makes about 3½ - 4 dozen

1 Cup	butter, softened
½ tsp.	almond extract
⅔ Cup	sugar
2 Cups	all-purpose flour
½ Cup	cherry jam/preserves or seedless raspberry jam

Glaze:

½ Cup	powdered sugar
½ tsp.	almond extract
1-1½ tsp.	water

Cream butter, extract, and sugar in a large bowl until light and fluffy.
Add flour and mix well. This may take a while, but it will come together.
Wrap dough in plastic wrap, chill the dough for 1 hour. Preheat oven to 350°.
Roll dough into 1 inch balls.
Place dough balls about 2 inches apart on greased or parchment-lined baking sheets.
Using the end of a wooden spoon handle, make an indentation in the center of each.
Fill each with about ¼ teaspoon of jam or preserves.
Bake 13-16 minutes, or until edges are lightly browned.
Remove from baking sheets to wire rack to cool completely.
For the glaze:
In a small bowl combine sugar, extract, and 1 teaspoon of the water.
Add the remaining water a little at a time until you achieve a nice drizzling consistency.
Drizzle glaze over cooled cookies using the edge of a butter knife dipped in the icing.
Drizzle in several directions. A fork will work as well, I just prefer the knife.
Let drizzle dry before serving or packaging.

Cranberry-Orange Biscotti

I make this every Christmas as a gift for my best girlfriend Jean. It has become a tradition.

Makes about 3 dozen

⅔ Cup	sugar
½ Cup	vegetable oil
1½ Tblsp.	fresh grated orange peel (make sure to wash the orange first)
2 tsp.	vanilla
2	large eggs
2½ Cups	all-purpose flour
¾ Cup	dried cranberries, chopped (if you can find the orange flavored ones, even better)
1 tsp.	baking powder
¼ tsp.	salt
¼ tsp.	baking soda

Preheat oven to 350°.

Mix sugar, oil, orange peel, vanilla, and eggs in a large bowl.

Stir in remaining ingredients.

On a lightly floured surface, knead until smooth. Shape into two 10 X 3 inch rectangles.

Place side by side on an ungreased or parchment-lined baking sheet.

Bake 25-30 minutes, or until toothpick comes out clean when inserted in center.

Cool on baking sheet about 15 minutes.

Cut each rectangle crosswise into about ½ inch slices.

Place, cut side down on cookie sheet (you may need to use more than one baking sheet for this part of the recipe).

Bake about 15 minutes, flipping to other side about half way through. The biscotti should be crisp and lightly browned.

Remove right away to wire rack.

Eggnog Crème Brûlée

This recipe sounds difficult, but really is not. If you love eggnog, you will love this dessert. A creamy, rich base under a crispy sugary top layer.

Makes 4 servings

1½ Cups	whipping cream
3	egg yokes
1	egg
¼ Cup	sugar
½ tsp.	rum extract
1 tsp.	vanilla
¼ tsp.	nutmeg
¼ Cup	packed brown sugar

Preheat oven to 325°.
Place four 6-oz. ramekins or custard cups in a 9 by 9 inch baking pan.
Heat whipping cream in a small saucepan, just to a simmer.
Remove from heat.
In a medium bowl, combine egg yokes and egg. Beat well.
Stir in sugar with a wire whisk until combined.
Stir in hot whipping cream slowly until well blended.
Stir in rum extract, vanilla, and nutmeg.
Pour mixture into ramekins.
Place baking pan in oven.
Pour hot water into pan until it is about ¾ the height of the ramekins.
Bake for 30-35 minutes or until centers are set.
Remove from oven.
Place cups on a wire rack to cool.
Using a spatula under each cup makes it easier to remove the ramekins from the hot water.
Cool 30 minutes.
Refrigerate at least 4 hours, or overnight.
Before serving, place ramekins in the 9 by 9 pan.
Top each with 1 Tblsp. of the brown sugar. Spread out over the tops.
Put under broiler 1 to 2 minutes, or until the sugar starts to bubble and melt.
Store in refrigerator.

Graham Cracker Torte

This simple, no-bake torte looks like something that you spent hours making, once you slice it. Can be done using other colored gelatin. I do this one in Green and Gold sometimes for football gatherings.

14	full-sized graham crackers (all 4 squares)
¾ Cup	applesauce
1	4-serving package of gelatin in cherry flavor
¾ Cup	applesauce
1	4-serving package of gelatin in lime flavor

½ of an 8-oz. container of frozen whipped topping, thawed
½ Cup powdered sugar
colored sugars or sprinkles to garnish

In one bowl, mix the first ¾ cup of applesauce with the dry cherry gelatin and mix well.
In another bowl, mix the second ¾ cup of applesauce with the dry lime gelatin and mix well.
Line up 2 of the graham crackers end on end, narrow ends together, forming a long rectangle on a long narrow platter or foil-covered heavy cardboard.
Spread with 2 heaping tablespoons of one color applesauce mixture.
Spread evenly and almost to the edges.
Place 2 graham crackers on top of that, making sure to try to keep the stack straight.
Press down just a little bit, to help spread the applesauce to the edges.
So the same with the other color of applesauce.
Repeat alternating colors of applesauce in the layers.
Last layer is graham crackers.
You should have 3 layers of red filling, 3 layers of green filling.
Cover loosely with plastic wrap and refrigerate for about 2 hours to let set.
Mix the whipped topping with the powdered sugar.
Frost the sides and top of the cake.
Frost the sides with a thin layer first, then a thicker layer to avoid getting too much of the gelatin mixture in the frosting.
Refrigerate overnight.
If desired, sprinkle a little colored sugar or sprinkles on top before slicing.
Cut in slices crosswise to serve.
The gelatin and applesauce mixture softens the graham crackers into a very nice soft torte.

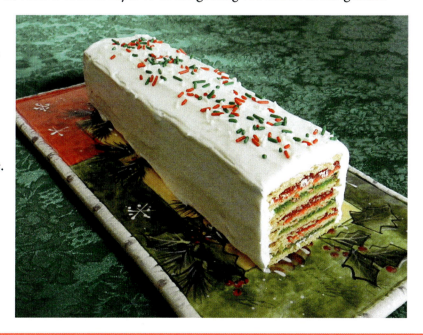

Sweet Potato Pie

Something this good should be eaten all year! A wonderful recipe from my friend Yolanda Webb.

1	9 inch unbaked pie shell, homemade or store-bought
1 lb.	sweet potatoes
½ Cup	butter, softened
1 Cup	sugar
½ Cup	evaporated milk, or heavy cream
2	eggs
1 tsp.	vanilla

cinnamon and nutmeg to taste (I use 1 tsp. cinnamon and ¼ tsp. nutmeg)

Preheat ovenn to 350°.

Boil the sweet potatoes for 40-50 minutes, until fork tender.

Run cold water over the potatoes to cool, and remove the skin by hand.

Break apart in a bowl. Use a hand mixer to beat until smooth. Remove any visible strings.

Go through it with a fork to make sure you have all of the obvious strings out.

Add the butter and mix well with the mixer.

Sir in the sugar, milk, eggs, vanilla, cinnamon, and nutmeg.

Beat until smooth. Taste to see if more spices are needed.

Pour into the pie crust.

Bake for 55 to 60 minutes, or until knife inserted in the center comes out clean.

Pie may puff up a little like a souffle while baking, but will settle when cool.

Christmas Gifts & Candy

A Christmas Memory...150
Oyster Dillies...151
Cinnamon Pecans...152
Brown Bread...153
Peanut Butter Fudge...154
Mom's Best Fudge...155
Aloha Fudge...156

Christmas has always been very special to me, but the best gifts and memories that I received were not found in my stocking. They were the family, friends, and food that surrounded the holiday.

A Christmas Memory

During the Christmas holiday season, a lot of focus is put on gifts.
I could not tell you many of the gifts that I was given as a child, at least not the material ones.
What I do remember is the love that always surrounded me, especially during the holidays.
My parents, brothers, grandparents, aunts, uncles, and cousins were the best part of this season.
Also, the food. Mom busy for weeks in the kitchen making cookies and candy to give as gifts,
and for us if we were good.
The cookies and brown bread from my Grandma B., especially the gingerbread, my favorite.
Always a special dinner at one of our Grandma and Grandpa's houses.
Laying for hours looking at the lights and tinsel on the tree.
Hoping we would get one of the candy canes on Grandma's tree.
Watching the bubble lights, which seemed so magical to a child.
My gifts that I cherish most have not changed.
But, the list has grown to include:
Truly good friends and neighbors.
The best in-laws that a woman could wish for.

Our 8 wonderful grandchildren.

Our 6 wonderful kids and their significant others.

And of course, my wonderful husband, the love of my life.

Oyster Dillies

This is an easy recipe, no baking required, that Mom makes a lot for gifts.

2	brown paper grocery bags, double bagged, make sure the inside bag is a brand new one
2	12-13-oz. packages of oyster crackers
1 pkg.	dry Hidden Valley Ranch Dressing, original, not buttermilk
¼ tsp.	garlic powder
1 Tblsp.	dried dillweed
1 tsp.	lemon pepper
1 Cup	vegetable oil

Put crackers in double, clean brown paper bag.

Mix rest of ingredients in a bowl.

Pour over crackers in bag. Shake for 1 minute. Pour into air tight container.

Ready to eat in 15 minutes.

Will last about a week. Be careful, these are addictive.

Cinnamon Pecans

Making these not only gives you something wonderful to gift, or to eat yourself, but will make your house smell wonderful.

1	egg white
1 lb.	(4 cups) pecan halves
½ Cup	granulated sugar
¼ tsp.	salt
2 tsp.	cinnamon

Preheat oven to 275°.
Beat egg white in a large bowl with a whisk until foamy. Add rest of ingredients and stir with a spoon until pecans are coated.
Bake 30 minutes in a 9 by 13 dish stirring every 10 minutes during baking time. Spread on wax paper to cool. Store in an airtight container.
I like to add ⅓ cup of sweetened dried cranberries, as well as ⅓ cup of some kind of baking chip (white chocolate, milk chocolate, peanut butter, butterscotch), or whatever you like.

Brown Bread

My grandma B used to make this every year for Christmas to give along with her Christmas cookies. As a child, I always thought that the bread was named after her, as her last name was a different spelling of Brown, until I discovered that it was named after the dark brown color of the bread. This is a neat recipe that is baked in soup cans, the size that condensed soup comes in.

Makes 5 loaves

2 Cups	water
1¾ Cup	raisins
1¼ Cups	packed brown sugar
1 Tblsp.	butter, softened
1	egg, slightly beaten
3½ Cups	flour, sifted
2 tsp.	baking soda
1 tsp.	salt
1 tsp.	vanilla
½ Cup	chopped walnuts, if desired

Bring the water to a boil in a saucepan, add the raisins and boil for 5 minutes.
Let cool completely.
In a large bowl, cream the brown sugar and butter.
Add the egg and mix well.
Add the cooled raisin and water mixture. Mix well.
Sift the flour, baking soda, and salt together into the raisin mixture. Mix well.
Add the vanilla and walnuts, if using.

Preheat oven to 350°.
Spray the insides of 5 condensed soup sized cans .
Divide the batter between the cans.
Place on a tray in oven for 50 minutes.
Dough will fill the can and bake just a little above the top of the can in a rounded shape.

Let bread sit in the can for 5 minutes, then turn the cans upside down to remove.
Let cool on a cooling rack. I stand them upright.

These are great cut in slices with a little butter, honey butter, or cream cheese.

Peanut Butter Fudge

If you love the flavor of chocolate and peanut butter together, you will love this recipe.

1 Cup peanut butter chips
1½ Cups semisweet chocolate chips
1 14-oz. can of sweetened condensed milk
2 Tblsp. butter or margarine, softened
1 tsp. vanilla

Line a 9 inch baking pan with foil or plastic wrap. Spray very lightly with cooking spray.
In a 4-cup microwavable measuring cup, or other microwaveable bowl, put all the ingredients except the vanilla.
Microwave for 1-2 minutes on high, stirring every 30 seconds, until chips are melted.
Add vanilla and stir.
Pour into prepared pan.
Cover and refrigerate for 2 hours.
Lift out of pan by the foil or plastic wrap.
Cut into squares.

Another fun thing to do with this fudge is to give as special gifts:
Get 5-6 new 3 inch metal cookie cutters that are an inch or so high.
Form a piece of foil about 5 inches square around the back and sides of the cutters.
The foil is to keep the fudge from leaking out the bottom as much as possible.
Place the prepared cutters on a baking sheet.
Spray the insides of the cutters with cooking spray.
Pour, or spoon the hot fudge into the cutters, filling to the top and smoothing the top.
Let refrigerate for at least 2 hours.
Decorate with frosting and candies of choice.
Remove the foil from the cutters.
Remove any excess fudge from the outside of the cutters.
Once the frosting is dry, place the cutter into a plastic bag and tie with a ribbon.
The gift is not only the fudge, but a cute cookie cutter to use or hang on a tree.

Mom's Best Fudge

*Mom used to make this fudge every Christmas.
It was a prized treat during the Christmas holiday.*

4½ Cups sugar
¾ Cup   butter (1½ Sticks)
1   12-oz. can of evaporated milk (NOT sweetened condensed)
3 Cups   semisweet chocolate chips
1   7.5-oz. jar of marshmallow fluff
1 Cup   nuts, walnuts or pecans work best, if desired
1 tsp.   vanilla

Place the sugar, butter, and milk in a large kettle.
Heat on low stirring constantly.
Once mixture begins to boil, boil for 5 minutes, stirring constantly.
Remove from heat.
Stir in the chocolate chips and marshmallow fluff until all the chips are melted.
Add the nuts and vanilla.
Line two 9 inch baking pans with foil, spray with cooking spray.
Divide the fudge between the 2 trays and smooth top with a spoon.
Let cool, then cover and put in the refrigerator.
Refrigerate for at least 4 hours.
To remove from pan, lift out with the foil, this makes removal and cutting much easier.
Hint: Try to use pans with square, rather than rounded corners so that you get nicer pieces out of the corners.

Aloha Fudge

If someone on your gift list loves the tastes of the tropics, this would be a perfect gift.

½ Cup	powdered sugar
3 oz.	cream cheese, softened
½ Cup	canned vanilla frosting, Pillsbury Creamy Supreme works best (do not use whipped frosting)
1	12-oz. bag white chocolate chips, use a good quality chip
¾ Cup	chopped macadamia nuts
⅔ Cup	dried pineapple, cut in about ¼ inch pieces.
⅓ Cup	shredded coconut

Line a 9 inch baking pan with foil.
Spray lightly with cooking spray.
Mix the powdered sugar, cream cheese, and frosting in a medium bowl. Mix well.
If the nuts are not chopped, put them in a zippered bag and crush with a rolling pin. They don't need to be too small, just not halves or whole, to make slicing the fudge easier.
Melt the white chocolate chips in a saucepan stirring constantly until chips are melted.
Pour over the cream cheese mixture.
Add the nuts, pineapple, and coconut. Mix well.
Pack into the prepared pan.
Pat down and into all the corners (I use a sandwich bag with a little cooking spray on it to do this).
Refrigerate for at least 1 hour until firm.
Lift out of tray using the foil, and cut into squares.
Serve at room temperature, but store any that is left in the refrigerator.

Year-Round Family Foods

We enjoy our life in the country all year-round. You never know what will be flying overhead. These beautiful hot air ballons fly over all year, even on warm winter days. Someday, I hope that they land and say, "Hi."

Veggies...160
Chicken, Beef, and Pork...168
Seafood...179
Basics...188
Desserts...192

Veggies

Vegetarian Enchiladas...161
Ravioli with Chickpeas and Veggies...162
Fried Corn...163
Cajun Sweet Potatoes...164
Baked Breaded Eggplant...165
Grilled Veggie Medley...166
Stuffed Acorn Squash...167

Even this squirrel enjoys his vegetables.

Vegetarian Enchiladas

Having a son who is vegan, we have experimented with some of our family dishes made over for him. This is one of those meals.

1 Tblsp. olive oil
6 oz. vegan meat crumbles
salt and pepper
½ tsp. chili powder
1 15-oz. can of vegetarian chili
1 8-oz. can of tomato sauce
⅓ Cup onions, chopped
6 slices of vegan cheese, unwrapped and cut into thirds
8 corn tortillas

Preheat oven to 375°.
Brown vegan crumbles in a frying pan, in the olive oil.
Salt and pepper to taste.
Add chili powder, can of chili, and tomato sauce to browned crumbles.
heat on low for about 5 minutes. Stir frequently.
Heat tortillas on a paper plate in the microwave, just enough to soften.
Spray an 8 by 8 or 9 by 9 inch baking pan with cooking spray.
Place first tortilla at side of pan and fill with 1½ - 2 tablespoons of the chili mixture.
Top with a sprinkle of chopped onions and one of the strips of cheese.
Fold tortilla over itself to make a tube shape.
Continue until pan is full, or tortillas are all used.
Top each with another strip of cheese.
Sprinkle with remaining chopped onions.
Add about ¼ cup of water to remaining chili mixture, heat.
Pour remaining chili mixture over the top and spread out.
Cover with foil and seal tightly.
Bake for 30-35 minutes.
Let cool a little before serving.

Ravioli with Chickpeas and Veggies

Makes 2 nice-sized servings

2 Cups	frozen or fresh spinach ravioli, cooked as directed (or any other flavor ravioli you might like)
2 Cups	fresh seasonal veggies of your choice (I used pepper and asparagus in this one)
⅓ Cup	chopped onion (red, yellow, white, whichever you like)
1	15-oz. can of chickpeas, also known as garbanzo beans, drained and rinsed
1 Tblsp.	olive oil
½ Cup	chopped tomato

¼ Cup of your favorite pesto, store bought or home made
salt to taste
Parmesan cheese to garnish (whatever you have, shredded or grated, does not matter)

Cut the fresh veggies into bite-size pieces.
Heat the olive oil in a large skillet. Saute the fresh veggies and onion until tender crisp.
Add the chickpeas about half way through to warm and get a little crispy on the outside.
Stir in the chopped tomatoes. Toss with the pesto.
Check the salt level. You might not need any depending upon the saltiness level of the pesto.
Place the cooked ravioli on a plate, top with the veggie/chickpea mixture.
Garnish with the Parmesan, if desired.

Fried Corn

A great way to use some of the ears of corn from the garden, or you can use frozen corn kernels. This is a great side dish for chicken or pork. Frying the corn makes it even sweeter.

2-3	pieces of bacon, cut in squares
2 Tblsp.	olive oil
3 Cups	corn cut off of the cob, or frozen corn.
¼	large red onion, chopped
½	green pepper, chopped
1 Cup	tomato, chopped

salt and pepper to taste

In a large frying pan, cook the bacon until crispy, no need to drain the fat.
Add the Olive oil.
Add the corn, onion, and pepper. Fry on low, stirring every few minutes. When the corn looks slightly browned, add the tomato and cook until heated through.
Season to taste with salt and pepper.

Cajun Sweet Potatoes

This is such a wonderful, 3-ingredient dish. We make it at least 4 times a month at our house.
A great side dish for chicken or pork.
The sweet of the sweet potato and the kick of the Cajun seasoning is what makes this one work.

Makes 2-3 servings

1   large sweet potato
olive oil
Cajun seasoning

Preheat oven to 375°.
Peel the sweet potato and cut in ¼ inch slices either using a knife or a crinkle cutter.
Line a baking pan with sides with foil and spray with cooking spray.
Lay the cut sweet potato slices in a single layer on the baking pan.
Drizzle with olive oil and sprinkle with Cajun seasoning.
Bake until the potatoes are soft when checked with a fork, and maybe the edges starting to get a little dark.
Yes, this recipe is that easy, but oh, so tasty!

Baked Breaded Eggplant

This recipe can be used in so many ways:
On a bun with marinara sauce, mozzarella cheese, and sauteed onion, mushrooms, and peppers.
As a base for individual pizzas with pizza sauce, your favorite toppings, and cheese.
Or, as a simple eggplant parmesan, by putting over cooked spaghetti with marinara sauce and mozzarella on top.

1	large eggplant, ends removed, peeled, and cut into ½ inch slices.
1	egg, beaten with 2 tsp. water
1 Cup	panko bread crumbs (gluten free can be used)
1 Tblsp.	Italian seasoning
½ tsp.	salt
2 Tblsp.	grated Parmesan cheese

Preheat oven to 400°.

Prepare the eggplant. Put the egg in a bowl and whisk with the water. On a plate, mix the crumbs, seasoning, salt, and cheese together.

Line a large pan with sides with foil, spray with cooking spray.

Dip each slice of eggplant in the egg and water combo, making sure both sides and edges are dipped. Roll in the crumb mixture, patting the mixture on to make sure it is coated.

Place the breaded eggplant in a single layer on the prepared pan.

Bake for 15 minutes on one side, flipping for an additional 10-15 minutes, until crispy and starting to brown.

These are good just as is, or in one of the suggested recipes above.

They can be frozen after baking:

Just put a single layer on a baking sheet in the freezer. Once frozen, put in a container with wax paper in between layers. Can be baked from the frozen state until hot and crisp, at about 350°.

Grilled Veggie Medley

If you love oven roasted vegetables, grilling them takes them up just a little higher on the flavor scale. In addition to the vegetables that I used in my mixture, you could do eggplant, zucchini, or yellow squash, whatever is in season.
Whenever I make these, I like to make extra. I like having the heated vegetables in a whole grain tortilla with a sprinkle of feta or Parmesan cheese for a nice light lunch.

Makes 1 serving:

1½ Cups mixed fresh vegetables (I used asparagus spears, red onion strips, green pepper strips, and mushrooms, quartered or cut in half)
1 tsp.   olive oil
a sprinkle of salt and pepper

Toss the vegetables with the oil. Using a grilling pan made for vegetables or fish, grill until lightly charred and starting to get tender, stirring as needed.

Or, to roast in the oven, line a pan with foil and spray with nonstick spray. Roast at 425°, stirring as needed until charred and just starting to get tender.

Sprinkle with salt and pepper to taste.

Stuffed Acorn Squash

A very flavorful side dish, one of our favorites.

Makes 2 servings

1	acorn squash
½ Cup	apples, chopped
½ Cup	walnuts or pecans, chopped
3 Tblsp.	brown sugar
1 Tblsp.	butter or margarine

Preheat oven to 375°.

Cut acorn squash in half lengthwise. Scoop out seeds and membrane. If halves do not sit well when placed cut side up, a thin piece can be cut off of the back to help them not tip over.

Mix the apples, nuts, and brown sugar in a small bowl.

Fill both sides of the squash evenly with the mixture. Top each with half of the butter or margarine.

Place in a pan with sides, cut/filled side up. Put about an inch of water in the pan surrounding the squash.

Cover with foil and bake for about 1½ hours, checking periodically with a fork to see if they are soft.

Variations: Add 2 Tblsp. of coarsely chopped cranberries and add an extra tablespoon of brown sugar; or add 2 tablespoons of fresh raspberries.

Chicken, Beef, and Pork

Chicken Tostadas with Black Bean Salsa...169
Chicken Fajitas...170
Chicken Curry in the Slow Cooker...171
Italian Meatballs...172
Souper Burgers...173
Hubby's Easy Enchiladas...174
Stuffed Peppers...175
Cindy's Surprise Casserole...176
Slow Cooker Pot Roast...177
Baked Pork Chops...178

My grandma's pig and chicken salt and pepper sets.

Chicken Tostadas with Black Bean Salsa

2-4	boneless/skinless chicken breasts
1	4-oz. can mild diced green chiles
¼ tsp.	ground cumin per chicken breast
¼ Cup	water

flat tostada shells, crisped in the oven per package directions (we usually use 2 per serving)

1	16-oz. can refried beans, heated in a sauce pan

Put the first four ingredients in a crock pot for 6-8 hours on low.

Once the chicken can be easily shredded using 2 forks, you can do that right in the crock pot.

To assemble:

Lay one tostada shell on the plate, spread with about 2 tablespoons of refried beans, and about ¼ cup of the shredded chicken.

Then, top with your favorite toppings (lettuce, chopped tomatoes, chopped onions, shredded cheddar or taco cheese, chopped avocado, sliced black olives, sour cream, jalapeno slices), whatever you like.

If desired, serve with black bean salsa:

Black Bean Salsa

This is great as a side dish, or even makes a great vegetarian taco filling.

1	15-oz. can of black beans, drained and rinsed
¼ Cup	chopped, green, red, or yellow sweet pepper
¼ Cup	chopped onion, yellow, white, or red
¼ Cup	chopped tomato

zest from 1 small lime

¼ tsp.	ground cumin

salt to taste

Mix the above ingredients together and let chill for at least 2 hours.

Before serving, stir in any or all of these you desire:

½ chopped avocado
½ Cup chopped mango
½ minced jalapeno
¼ Cup whole kernel corn
1-2 teaspoons chopped cilantro

Chicken Fajitas

One of our favorites to make when we have fresh peppers in the garden, or, when a variety of colorful ones are reasonably priced at the market

Makes 4 large or 6-8 small fajitas

2 Tblsp.	olive oil
1 lb.	chicken breasts (boneless, skinless)
1/2	red onion cut into strips
1½ Cup	pepper strips (a mixture of several colors makes for the most colorful dish, but only one color can be used, if desired)

Fajita Seasoning:
2 tsp.	chili powder
1 tsp.	paprika
1 tsp.	ground cumin
¼ tsp.	garlic powder
1 tsp.	salt

a sprinkle of Cayenne powder (red pepper powder)

4 large or 6-8 small flour tortillas
your favorite toppings (we like chopped tomatoes, mashed avocado, and sour cream)

Cut the chicken breasts into strips. Helpful Hint: They cut easier when partially frozen.

Heat oil in a large skillet.

In a large bowl, combine the chicken, onion, and peppers.

Mix the spices in a small bowl, pour over the chicken and vegetables and stir well to coat everything.

Pour the seasoned chicken and vegetable mix into the large skillet where the oil has been heated.

Cover and simmer on low for about 5 minutes.

Uncover, turn up the heat to medium, and cook stirring frequently until chicken is cooked and vegetables become tender.

Heat tortillas on a griddle or in a large skillet.

Top with the meat mixture.

Garnish with your favorite toppings. Fold and eat.

Chicken Curry in the Slow Cooker

The first time that I tried this dish, my Forever Friend Jean Rohr (pictured with her husband, Randy) made it for me at lunch. It tasted like a dish that had really been difficult to make, but once she shared the recipe, I was amazed at how easy it was. Serve over brown rice, couscous, or pasta to take advantage of the wonderful sauce.
This time when I made it, I had some wonderful sweet potato egg noodles on hand from a local company. They tasted great with it.

Makes 8-10 servings
This makes a big batch, and recipe can be cut in half easily.

2½-3 lbs. boneless, skinless chicken breasts, cubed (this is much easier to do if chicken is partially frozen)
1 16-oz. jar of your favorite brand of thick and chunky salsa
1 onion, chopped
1-2 Tblsp. sweet curry powder, I prefer the sweet, as it is not so spicy, but gives plenty of flavor
1 Cup sour cream or plain Greek yogurt

Put the chicken in the slow cooker.
Mix the salsa, onion, and curry powder. You might want to start with the smaller amount to see how you like the curry flavor and add more later.
Add mixture to chicken in slow cooker. Cover the slow cooker.
Cook 8 hours on low or 4-5 hours on high.
Once cooked, stir in the sour cream or yogurt.
Serve over the starch of your choice.
Garnish with thinly sliced green onions, if desired.

171

Italian Meatballs

These are the meatballs that I always serve with my spaghetti.

2 lbs.	ground beef, we prefer ground chuck
½ Cup	chopped onions
1 Cup	dried bread crumbs
2 tsp.	Italian seasoning
2	eggs
1 tsp.	salt
½ tsp.	garlic powder

Preheat oven to 350°.

Mix all ingredients together well.

Form into about 1½ inch balls. Place on a baking sheet with sides, like a jelly roll pan, that has been lined with foil and sprayed with cooking spray.

Bake until they are starting to brown and meat is no longer pink, usually 20-30 minutes. I always make a test meatball or two to check if done.

Drain on paper towels and add to your spaghetti sauce before serving.

These can also be done ahead of time and reheated in the sauce. They also freeze great in a freezer bag or plastic storage container.

Souper Burgers

One of our favorite simple suppers, but oh so satisfying.

Makes 4 burgers

1 lb.	ground beef
¼ Cup	yellow or white onion, chopped
salt and pepper to taste	
1 Can	cream of mushroom soup
1 Can	cream of celery soup
¼ Cup	water
	OR for gluten free
1	18-oz. can of gluten free creamy mushroom soup
1 Cup	frozen peas

Mix ground beef, onion, and salt and pepper.
Form into 4 burgers.
Fry in a pan with higher sides, flipping to completely cook.
When burgers are cooked, add the soups and water, if doing gluten free, just use the gluten free soup (it is thinner and does not need to be thinned).
Simmer, covered for 10 minutes.
Add peas and cook just another minute.

We like to serve these on large biscuits or gluten free buns.
Make sure to serve with rice or egg noodles on the side to use up some of the sauce.

Hubby's Easy Enchiladas

This is a family favorite that my hubby Joel makes for many of the kids' birthday celebrations. We usually need to double the recipe and make 2 pans, as the kids love it, and love to take some home.

1 lb.	ground beef
salt and pepper	
1	15-oz. can chili without beans, we prefer Hormel brand
10 slices	wrapped american-style cheese, unwrapped and cut into thirds
½ Cup	onion, chopped
13-15	corn tortillas

Brown ground beef in a frying pan, drain some of the fat. Salt and pepper to taste.
Add can of chili to browned seasoned beef and heat on low for about 5 minutes.
Stir frequently.
Heat tortillas on a paper plate in the microwave, just enough to soften.
Preheat oven to 375°.
Spray a 9 by 13 inch baking pan with cooking spray.
Place first tortilla at side of pan and fill with 1½-2 tablespoons of the chili mixture.
Top with a sprinkle of chopped onions and one of the strips of cheese.
Fold tortilla over itself to make a tube shape.
Continue until pan is full, or tortillas are all used.
Top each with another strip of cheese.
Sprinkle with remaining chopped onions.
Add about ¼ cup of water to remaining chili mixture, heat.
Pour remaining chili mixture over the top and spread out.
Cover with foil and seal tightly.
Bake for 30-35 minutes.
Let cool a little before serving.

Stuffed Peppers

We like to serve these with corn on the cob, fresh sliced cucumbers and cherry tomatoes from the garden. All from the garden or farmers's market this time of year. But of course, these are great any time of year.

Makes 6 servings

6	large green peppers (red, yellow, orange can also be used) the peppers with 4 bumps at the bottom tend to sit best in the pan
3 Tblsp.	chopped onion
1 lb.	ground beef
¼ tsp.	garlic powder
1 tsp.	salt
1 Cup	cooked brown rice (you can use white, but we prefer brown)
3	8-oz. cans tomato sauce.
½-¾ Cup	shredded cheddar cheese

Preheat oven to 350°.
Cut the top off of each of the peppers, remove seeds and membrane.
Fill a large pan with water and bring to a boil. Boil the peppers for 5 minutes, drain.
Cook the onion and beef until almost browned, but still a little pink. Drain fat.
Add garlic powder, salt, rice, and 2 cans of tomato sauce.
Stir together and simmer until heated.
Place the peppers cut side up in an ungreased baking dish with sides.
Divide the stuffing mixture equally between the peppers.
Pour the last can of tomato sauce over the stuffed peppers equally.
Cover. Bake 45 minutes, uncover and bake for 15 minutes longer.
Sprinkle the cheese on top and bake for an additional 5 minutes.

Cindy's Surprise Casserole

This recipe is a favorite of my dear friend Cindy Koss and her husband Bill. More than 20 years ago, our family received a precious gift from Cindy, her daughter Brenda as our daughter-in-law, married to our son, Tim.
Cindy and I share two grandchildren, Tyler and Lillian.

This recipe is a cross between a cheeseburger and a shepard's pie.

1-1½ lbs.	ground chuck
½ tsp.	onion powder
½ tsp.	garlic powder
salt and pepper to taste	
1	can condensed cheddar cheese soup
6	servings of prepared instant potatoes

Preheat oven to 400°.

Brown ground chuck, drain.

Add onion powder, garlic powder, salt, and pepper.

Spray a 2 quart casserole dish with cooking spray.

Add the ground beef to the casserole dish.

Add about half of the can of soup to the ground beef, mix well.

Spread evenly over bottom of casserole dish.

If potatoes are too thin, add a few more flakes of instant potatoes to thicken up.

Spread potatoes evenly over the top of the meat layer.

Mix enough water with the rest of the can of soup to make a thick cheese sauce.

Pour the sauce over the mashed potato layer and spread evenly.

Bake for 35-45 minutes until cheese sauce is slightly browned.

Remove from oven and let sit for about 5 minutes before serving.

Helpful hint:
For holiday dinners we usually make homemade mashed potatoes, but having a package of instant potatoes on hand is a great way to "fix" homemade mashed potatoes that are too thin.
Just spoon some in until you achieve the desired consistency.

Slow Cooker Pot Roast

*This recipe was given to me by my dear friend Yolanda Webb.
It turns out very tender, and the sauce is wonderful over mashed potatoes.*

2   10.75-oz. cans cream of mushroom soup,
             OR, one larger can of gluten free creamy mushroom soup
1   1-oz. package of dry onion soup mix
4-5 lbs.   chuck roast
1¼ Cups water or 10.5-oz can of beef consume or beef stock
salt and pepper to taste.

Season pot roast on both sides with salt and pepper.
If possible, let roast marinade in seasoning overnight.
In a slow cooker, mix the mushroom soup, onion soup mix, and water or beef broth.
Place the roast in the slow cooker, spoon some of the soup over the roast.
Cook on low for 8 hours.
So tender, just cut off chunks, this is not a roast you can slice easily.
It is what I like to call a spoon roast, as you can cut it with a spoon.
Serve the sauce over mashed potatoes.

Baked Pork Chops

Sometimes a relationship starts with something simple, like an email to order cookies.
Then, it blossoms into a cherished friendship where that person feels more like family.
This is a recipe from one of those people in my life, Mrs. Yolanda Webb, shown with her wonderful husband Mr. Edward Webb.
Recipe is displayed on a plate that she gave me.

4	bone-in, thin pork chops
1	stack from a pack of Ritz crackers (or to make gluten free, a 5-oz. box of Ritz-style gluten free crackers)

a generous sprinkle of garlic salt
2   eggs, beaten
paprika, salt, and pepper
¼ Cup   butter

Preheat oven to 375°.
Crush the crackers into crumbs (I use a zipper bag and a rolling pin).
In a shallow bowl, put the bread crumbs and the garlic salt. Mix together.
Place the beaten eggs in another shallow bowl.
Spray a 9 by 13 inch pan with cooking spray.
Sprinkle each side of a pork chop with paprika, salt, and pepper.
Dip both sides of the pork chop in egg.
Coat both sides of the pork chop with the crumb mixture. Pat more on to completely cover.
Shake over the plate to remove excess and place in the prepared baking pan.
Repeat with the other pork chops, placing them in a single layer in the prepared pan.
Dot with the butter around and on top of the pork chops.
Cover with foil. Bake for 30 minutes.
Remove the cover and bake for 15 minutes more.

Seafood

Our Favorite Tuna Casserole...180
Salmon with Tangy Dill Sauce...181
Seafood Stew...182
Shrimp with Veggies...183
Quick Shrimp Fried Rice...184
Jamaican Shrimp and Rice...185
Shrimp Tacos...186
Cajun Shrimp with Sausage Skillet...187

One fish, two fish, red fish, blue fish.

Our Favorite Tuna Casserole

6 oz.	(by weight) dry egg noodles or gluten free egg noodle shaped like the smaller lasagna corte
1 tsp.	olive oil, butter, or margarine
⅓ Cup	chopped onion
1 Cup	coarsely chopped mushrooms of your choice
⅓ Cup	chopped red pepper

sprinkle of salt

½ Cup	frozen green peas
1	can cream of mushroom soup or gluten free creamy mushroom soup
½ Cup	sour cream

milk to make a total of 4 cups of sauce

1 tsp.	dried dill
½ tsp.	lemon pepper
¼ tsp.	salt
2	2.6-oz. packets of tuna, packed in water.
1 Cup	bread crumbs, crushed potato chips, or crushed canned onion or canned French fried onions (gluten free if desired)

a drizzle of olive oil if using bread crumbs

Preheat oven to 350°.

Cook pasta according to package directions, do not overcook, as they will cook more in the casserole.

When cooked, drain and rinse, put in a large bowl.

Put the oil (or melt the butter or margarine) in the pan that you used to cook the pasta. Saute the onion, mushroom, and red pepper until softened. Sprinkle with salt.

Add the peas, onion mixture, and tuna to the bowl.

Mix together the sour cream, soup, and enough milk to make a total of 4 cups sauce.

Add the dill, lemon pepper, and salt.

Pour into the bowl containing the pasta, vegetables, and tuna, and mix the sauce in well. It will be very moist, but no one likes a dry casserole.

Spray a 2 quart casserole dish with cooking spray and pour the casserole ingredients from the bowl into the prepared dish.

Top with the bread crumbs, chips, or canned onions.

If using the bread crumbs, drizzle with a little olive oil.

Bake for 30-45 minutes. The casserole is done when it is bubbling nicely and the topping has browned.

Let set for about 10 minutes before serving to let the sauce thicken up a little.

Salmon with Tangy Dill Sauce

One of my favorites to make any time of year, but especially during the Lenten season.

Makes 4 servings

Sauce:
- ¾ Cup   plain yogurt
- 1 Tblsp. green onion, chopped
- ½ tsp.   lemon zest
- 1 Tblsp. fresh lemon juice
- 1 tsp.   dried dill weed
- ½ tsp.   salt

Salmon:
- 4   6-oz. salmon fillets (If using frozen, defrost first)
- 2 Tblsp. olive oil
- ½ tsp.   salt
- ¼ tsp.   lemon pepper

Mix together sauce ingredients. Chill for at least an hour in refrigerator.

Heat oil in a large skillet. Season both sides of salmon with the salt and lemon pepper

Cook in oil for 6-8 minutes on each side until meat is flaky.

I like to cook on the meat side first, finishing on the skin side if the skin is still on, that way I can check the meat easier to see if it is done.

Serve the salmon with a large dollop of the sauce on top.

Seafood Stew

2 Tblsp.	olive oil
1	medium onion chopped
4 cloves	garlic, minced
1 lb.	flaky white fish (haddock, tilapia, or cod) cut into 1½ inch pieces
1	14-oz. can diced tomatoes
sprinkle-¼ tsp.	chipotle pepper powder (depending on how hot you like it)
2 Tblsp.	sliced pimento-stuffed green olives
1 Tblsp.	capers, rinsed
1 tsp.	dried oregano
½ tsp.	salt
½ cup	water, as needed
¼ to ½ lb.	shrimp, uncooked, shelled, tail off
1	avocado, chopped (optional)
cooked brown rice (optional)	

Heat oil in a Dutch oven over medium heat.

Add onion and cook, stirring occasionally, until softened, about 2 minutes.

Add garlic and stir while cooking, about 30 seconds.

Add fish, tomatoes with the juices, chipotle powder, olives, capers, oregano, and salt. Stir to combine.

Add up to ½ cup water if the mixture seems dry.

Cover and simmer for 20 minutes. Add the shrimp and cook until shrimp are pink.

Serve over brown rice in a bowl (if you want a heartier meal), garnish with chopped avocado if desired.

Excellent served with corn bread or cornmeal muffins.

Shrimp with Veggies

I have so much fun with my veggie spiralizer. If you don't have one, you might want to get one, or veggies are now showing up in the grocery store already spiralized (they look like spaghetti, and are kept in the refrigerated section or produce section of a lot of grocery stores). This is also gluten free, which is a bonus.

Makes 3-4 servings

1 Tblsp.	olive oil
½ Cup	red onion, chopped
2 Cups	sliced mushrooms of your choice
2 Cups	asparagus spears cut in about 2 inch lengths
½	red pepper cut into strips
1-2	cloves garlic, minced
2 Cups	spiralized zucchini
8 oz.	peeled, deveined, uncooked shrimp, medium-large sized
1 Tblsp.	lemon juice
2 Tblsp.	cold butter
¼ tsp.	garlic powder
¼ tsp.	lemon pepper
salt to taste	

Heat olive oil in a very large saucepan or Dutch oven.
Stir fry the onion, mushrooms, asparagus, and red pepper until tender crisp.
Add garlic, zucchini and shrimp and cook until shrimp are pink.
Make a well in the center of the stir fry, add the lemon juice, butter, and seasoning to the center and cook until the butter melts.
Toss to mix the veggies and shrimp with the sauce.

Quick Shrimp Fried Rice

I make this dish when we are craving Asian food but don't want to go out. A wonderful side dish for this is grilled pineapple slices.
You can use gluten free soy sauce.

2 Tblsp.	vegetable oil
½ Cup	carrots, finely chopped or shredded
½ Cup	onion, chopped
2 Cups	cooked white or brown rice, chilled
2	eggs, beaten
6 oz.	shrimp, cooked, peeled and deveined
⅔ Tblsp.	soy sauce
½ Cup	frozen green peas
1	green onion, sliced diagonally, for garnish

In a large frying pan heat the oil, add the carrots and onion, and stir fry until the carrots are almost soft.
Add the rice and cover.
Stir every 30 seconds or so, covering after each time to allow carrots to soften.
Once veggies are soft and rice starts to brown, remove cover and push veggies and rice to edges of pan.
Add the beaten eggs in the center and stir them until they are scrambled.
Stir the eggs into the rice mixture, add the shrimp, soy sauce, and peas. Mix well.
Heat covered for just a minute until shrimp is heated and peas are defrosted.
Garnish on plates with the green onion.

Jamaican Shrimp and Rice

This is a wonderful, flavorful, healthy dish that will make you think you are on vacation. We enjoyed the seasoning on the shrimp so much that we created our shrimp taco recipe (see page 186).

Makes 4 servings

2 Cups	cooked rice, white or brown, heated
1	15-oz. can of black beans, rinsed and drained
1	8-oz. can of crushed pineapple
½ Cup	salsa of your choice
1	mango, peeled and cubed
1 lb.	shrimp, uncooked, peeled and deveined
1½ tsp.	Jamaican jerk seasoning
3 Tblsp.	olive oil
juice of 1 lime	
1	avocado
⅓ Cup	sour cream, light can be used
¼ tsp.	salt

sliced green onion and lime wedges to garnish, if desired

Heat the rice.
In a medium saucepan, combine the beans, pineapple, salsa, and mango. Heat.
Combine the shrimp with the Jamaican jerk seasoning. Stir until coated.
Heat the oil in a large skillet.
Cook the shrimp, stirring and turning frequently until the shrimp is pink on both sides, do not overcook. Squeeze the lime juice over the shrimp.
Mix avocado with sour cream and salt.
In each bowl, but ½ Cup of the heated rice. Place ¼ of the bean mixture on the other side of the bowl.
Put ¼ of the shrimp down the middle. Top with the avocado/sour cream mixture and garnish with the green onions and lime.

Shrimp Tacos

Lots of flavor in this simple dish

Makes 6 tacos

1 Tblsp.	olive oil
8 oz.	shrimp, medium sized, uncooked, shelled and deveined
1 tsp.	Jamaican jerk seasoning
6	corn tortillas
1	avocado, mashed
⅓ Cup	sour cream

salt and pepper to taste
1½ Cups shredded romaine or iceberg lettuce
½ Cup tomato, chopped
⅓ Cup onion, chopped
salsa and/or lime, optional

Heat the oil in a large saute pan.
Coat the shrimp with the seasoning by stirring together in a small bowl.
Saute seasoned shrimp until pink and fully cooked.
In a dry frying pan, heat the corn tortillas on both sides until they start to blister a little.
Mix avocado with sour cream and salt.
Divide the lettuce, tomato, and onion between the tortillas, divide the shrimp between the tortillas.
Top with avocado mixture.
If desired, drizzle with a little salsa and/or a squeeze of lime juice.

Cajun Shrimp with Sausage Skillet

We love this dish, a great way to use leftover rice.

Makes about 4 very generous servings.

¼ Cup	olive oil
12-16 oz.	smoked sausage or Andouille sausage, sliced thinly on the diagonal
3 cloves	garlic, finely chopped
1	small onion, cut in half, then thinly sliced
1	large green, red, or yellow pepper, thinly sliced (or a combination of 2 or more)
2 Cups	broccoli florets, cut into smaller pieces for faster cooking
1	8-oz. can tomato sauce
½ Cup	water
3 Cups	cooked rice (white or brown, whichever you prefer)
1 tsp.	Cajun seasoning
6-8 oz.	shrimp, medium to large, peeled and deveined

Heat oil in a large skillet. Add the sausage and cook until lightly browned.

Add the garlic and cook for about 30 seconds.

Add the pepper, onion, broccoli, tomato sauce, and water.

Simmer for about 10 minutes until vegetables are tender.

Stir in rice.

In a small bowl, mix the Cajun seasoning with the shrimp.

Put the shrimp on top of the skillet ingredients, cover, and cook until shrimp are pink, stirring every minute or so, it won't take long for the shrimp to cook.

Basics

Pie Crust...189
Home-Baked Croutons...190
Crockpot Stock...191

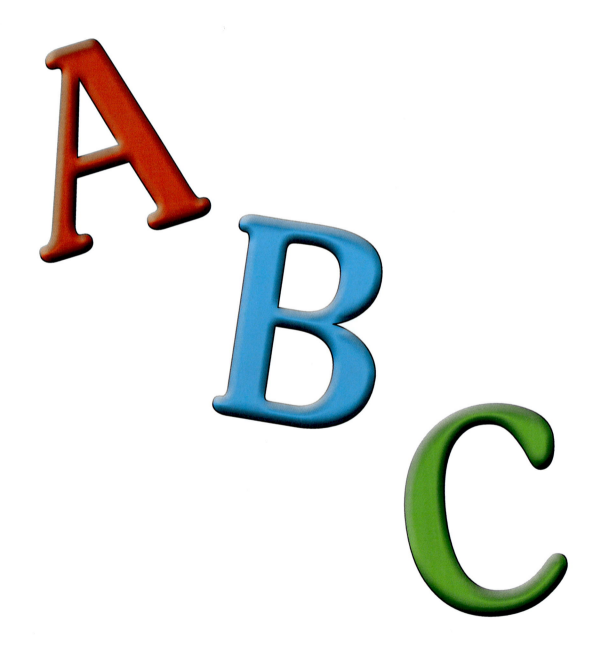

Pie Crust

This is the recipe that I have always used. I have made it using Namaste gluten free flour, as well as all purpose flour, and it turned out fine.

Makes two 8 inch or 9 inch pie crusts

2 Cups   flour
1 tsp.   salt
⅔ Cup plus 2 Tblsp. shortening
4-5 Tblsp. ice water

Measure flour and salt into a bowl. Cut in the shortening thoroughly.
Add water 1 tablespoon at a time until all of the flour is moistened and dough does not stick to side of bowl. Gluten free flour may require a little more water.
Shape into a ball and wrap in plastic wrap until ready to use.

Home-Baked Croutons

Whenever we have leftover hamburger or hot dog buns, this is one of my favorite ways to use them. I love croutons on salads, but they can be a little hard on the teeth. This makes amazing croutons that might not even make it to a salad, some of our kids and grandkids like munching on them as a snack.

This is really more of a method than a recipe, as it depends upon how many, and what kind of buns you have. The buns that I like to use are the cheap hamburger and hot dog buns, they seem to work best.

leftover hamburger or hot dog buns
olive oil
seasoning of your choice (I like to use garlic powder on some, Cajun seasoning on others)

Line a baking pan with sides with aluminum foil or parchment paper.
Separate the top of the bun from the bottom. This will make it much easier to separate into cubes once you are done cutting them.

    For hamburger buns, I cut each half of a bun once down the middle, then cut each half down the middle. Then, turn it and cut each the same way crosswise, making 16 cubes out of each half.

    For hot dog buns, I cut each in half once down the middle lengthwise, then crosswise once down the middle and twice crosswise on each side of the middle, making 12 cubes.

I spread the cubes on the lined baking pan, drizzle with olive oil, and bake at 300°. You need to watch these when getting towards the end, as they can go from golden brown and perfectly crispy to over-baked quickly. You will want to taste-test to make sure that they are crispy all the way through, as you don't want a soft center. Once you pull them from the oven, sprinkle the seasoning of choice over them. Let them cool completely before storing in a zippered bag.

Once you make these, you will never want store-bought ones again.

Crockpot Stock

Whenever we cut the meat off of a rotisserie or uncooked chicken, there are always those wonderful bones left. You can also do this with turkey. Wasting food is not something that I like to do, so, this is what I do:

1   **chicken carcus**
1   **onion, peeled and cut into quarters**
1   **large carrot, cut into chunks; or a handful of the baby carrots**
several stalks of celery, I like using the leafy ends

I put the chicken carcus and vegetables in the crockpot and fill with water until it is about an inch from the cover.
Put the setting on high until the water starts to boil, then set on low either overnight or all day (8-12 hours).
Once it is a nice golden yellow color, take the cover off. Let cool.
Put a large plastic container in the sink with a colander over it.
Pour the cooled stock into the colander.
I do this process in the sink, just in case I have misjudged the size of the container needed.
That way there is no mess over the counter.
Also, don't do like I have done on several occasions and forget to put the plastic container under the colander, all of my stock went right down the drain.
Discard the bones and vegetables, they are just for flavoring the broth.
I don't add any seasoning, as it depends what I will be using the broth for.
Put on the lid of the plastic container and chill in the refrigerator.
Once fully chilled, use a large spoon to remove any hardened fat from the top of the stock.
Put into freezer bags, I like to put it in 2-cup portions. Store in the freezer.
This stock is great for making soup or for cooking rice to add flavor.

To make a vegetable broth, just leave the bones out.

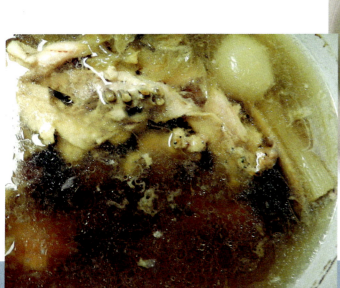

Desserts

Marble Cake Memory...193
Bananas Foster...194
Lemon Raspberry Cheesecake Bars...195
Blender Chocolate Mousse...196
Nunnie's Sour Cream Coffee Cake..197
Orange Sugar Cookies...198
Mom's Super Simple Doughnuts...199
Diane's Famous Chocolate Chip,
    Oatmeal, Cranberry, Walnut Cookies...200
Mom's Chocolate Yeast Cake...201
Sugar Cut-Out Cookies...202
My Vanilla Sugar Cookie Frosting...203

Grandma B's old baking tools help give me inspiration.

Marble Cake Memory

Usually when I make marble cake, I use a mix. However, my paternal grandma, who we called Nunnie, made hers from scratch.

When I was little, we lived above my grandparents in a duplex. I liked going downstairs to visit, especially when Nunnie was cooking. Watching and "helping" were my favorite things to do.

During one of those sessions, she was making a marble cake. I asked if I could help, and she said, "Yes."

My response was " I'll be back in a minute."

I went upstairs and returned soon with my jar of marbles. "We can use these," I told Nunnie.

I had never seen her laugh so hard.

After she stopped laughing, she explained to me what a marble cake really was.

I can never bake one without thinking of her.

Make sure to spend some time in the kitchen with your children and grandchildren. You never know what kind of memories you will be making.

Nunnie and Gramps

Bananas Foster

My version of a famous dessert, but no alcohol and no flambé, just lots of good flavor.
A simple, elegant, tasty dessert that requires no baking and is very inexpensive to make.

Makes 3-4 servings

2½ Tblsp.	butter
¼ Cup	brown sugar, packed
¼ tsp.	cinnamon
3	bananas, not too ripe, but not green, peeled and sliced in about ½ to ¾ inch slices

ice cream to serve it over, we like vanilla or butter pecan
whipped topping to garnish

Melt butter in a saute pan.
Add brown sugar and cinnamon. Cook and stir until melted and bubbly.
Add the banana slices.
Cook, stirring gently, until banana slices are coated and heated.
Serve the bananas and brown sugar sauce over ice cream and garnish with whipped cream.

Lemony Raspberry Cheesecake Bars

Loving the flavors of lemon and raspberry together, this is one of my favorites.

½ Cup	butter, softened
½ Cup	sugar
1⅓ Cup	all-purpose flour
½ Cup	sugar
1	8-oz. package cream cheese, softened
1 tsp.	vanilla
1	egg
1 tsp.	fresh lemon zest (about half of a lemon)
2 tsp.	fresh lemon juice
2 Tblsp.	seedless raspberry jam

Preheat oven to 350°.
Spray a 9 inch square pan with cooking spray.
In a large bowl combine the first ½ cup of sugar with the butter until well blended.
Add flour and mix until crumbly.
Press into the bottom of prepared pan.
Bake for 15-20 minutes until edges are golden brown.
In a large bowl, combine the sugar, cream cheese, vanilla, egg, zest and juice. Beat well.
Once crust is ready to take out of oven, remove and spread the cream cheese mixture evenly over crust.
Stir the first 2 tablespoons of the raspberry jam to loosen up.
Drop small spoonfuls over the top of the cream cheese mixture.
Using a small spoon or butter knife, swirl the jam into the cheese mixture to get a marbled effect.
Be careful not to disturb the crust.
Bake for 15-20 minutes until center of filling is set.
Cool 30-40 minutes.
Microwave remaining 2 tablespoons of jam in a small bowl for about 10 seconds.
Stir and spread over the top of the finished cheesecake like a glaze.
Refrigerate for 30 minutes.
Slice into 16 squares and store in refrigerator.

Blender Chocolate Mousse

A wonderful, chocolaty, fluffy treat, and so easy to make.
Garnish with your favorite berries and whipped cream, if desired.

1 Cup	semisweet chocolate chips
1	large egg, room temperature
1 tsp.	vanilla
1 Cup	heavy cream

Place chocolate chips, egg, and vanilla in blender and chop.
Heat cream in a small saucepan until very hot and small bubbles appear on the edge.
Do not boil, watch carefully.
With blender running, pour in the hot cream.
Blend until chocolate is melted and mixture is smooth.
Pour into loaf pan, cover with plastic wrap, and chill overnight.
Use a spoon or ice cream scoop to spoon into a pretty serving dish.
Or use a piping bag to pipe into a dish, that is what I did.
Garnish as desired.

Nunnie's Sour Cream Coffee Cake

My paternal grandma preferred to be called Nunnie, so it was always Nunnie and Gramps. She was a great baker, and as we lived upstairs from them when I was younger, the smells from her kitchen were enjoyed very often. You can always tell how good a recipe is by how worn the recipe itself is.

2 Cups	flour
1 tsp.	baking soda
1 tsp.	baking powder
a pinch of salt	
1 Cup	sugar
12 Tblsp. (1½ sticks) margarine, or as she called it, oleo	
2	eggs
1 Cup	sour cream
1 tsp.	vanilla
¼ Cup	sugar
½ Cup	chopped pecans or walnuts
¾ tsp.	cinnamon

Preheat oven to 350°.
Grease a 9 inch spring form pan.
Sift the flour, baking soda, baking powder, and salt together 4 times.
I do this by sifting from one bowl to another.
When done sifting, use the second bowl to cream the sugar and margarine together.
Mix in the eggs and sour cream.
Pour the sifted dry ingredients into the wet ingredients and mix well.
Mix the vanilla, sugar, nuts, and cinnamon together.
Pour half of the batter into the prepared spring form pan.
Spread to the edges with a spoon and level off.
Sprinkle the nut mixture over the batter.
Top with the remaining half of the batter .
Spread to the edges and level off.
Bake for 45 minutes.
Let cool for 10 minutes.
Loosen and remove the sides of the spring form pan. Let cool a little on a wire rack. You can leave the bottom of the spring form pan underneath.
You can use a large spatula to work under the cake to get it off of the spring form pan bottom and transfer to a serving platter, if desired.Cut in wedges, like a cake, to serve. Best served warm, or reheated for a few seconds in a microwave.

Orange Sugar Cookies

One of my favorite cookies that mom used to do at Halloween.
I like to make them during the summer as well, the citrus flavor lends itself to both times of year.

Number of cookies is dependent upon the size cutter used.

⅔ Cup	shortening
1¼ Cup	sugar
2	eggs, well beaten

Several drops of orange food color gel
3 Cups	all-purpose flour
1 tsp.	salt
2 tsp.	baking powder

grated zest from 1 orange
2-4 Tblsp. orange juice (from the grated orange)
granulated sugar, if desired

Preheat oven to 325°.
Line cookie sheets with parchment paper.
Cream shortening and sugar together.
Add eggs.
Mix in orange food color gel, a drop at a time, until you achieve a nice dark orange color.
Add flour, salt, and baking powder. Mix well.
Add the orange zest and the orange juice a tablespoon at a time until you achieve a nice consistency to the dough.
Wrap in plastic wrap and refrigerate for about 4 hours.
Roll out on a lightly floured surface to about ¼ inch thickness.
Cut out in the desired shape with a floured cookie cutter.
If desired, sprinkle with a little granulated sugar before baking.
Bake 12-15 minutes until set, but not brown.
Let cool on a wire rack.

Mom's Super Simple Doughnuts

Mom would bake these when we needed something sweet, simple, and quick.

Makes 5

1	5-pack of the small, refrigerated biscuits in the can, if you only can find a 10-pack, just double the recipe for the coating and make the 10
2 Tblsp.	butter or margarine, melted
3 Tblsp.	cinnamon sugar

Preheat oven to 350°.
Spray the insides of a standard-sized muffin tin with non-stick spray.
Open and separate the biscuits.
Dip each biscuit in the melted butter or margarine on all sides.
Roll in the cinnamon/sugar mixture.
I find using a short ramekin or cup for both the melted butter or margarine and the cinnamon sugar works easiest.
Place each coated biscuit into one of the muffin cups.
Finish until they are all coated.
Bake for 10-13 minutes until done.
When done they should be somewhat firm to the touch.
They will also be slightly brown, but it is hard to tell with the cinnamon/sugar.
Remove from muffin cups with a spoon and put on a cooling rack.
Good either cold and warm, but I like them warm best.

Diane's Famous Chocolate Chip, Oatmeal, Cranberry, Walnut Cookies

The name of this recipe is a mouthful, but so are these wonderful cookies. My dear friend Diane Burmeister, also my helping hand in the bakery for many years, shared this recipe with me.
Combining two favorites, chocolate chip and oatmeal cookies, it is a great combo.

Makes about 4 dozen, depending on size

¾ Cup	shortening
¾ Cup	brown sugar
¾ Cup	sugar
2	eggs
1 tsp.	vanilla
1 tsp.	boiling water
1½ Cups	flour
1 tsp.	baking soda
2 Cups	oatmeal
⅔ Cup	chocolate chips
1 Cup	chopped walnuts
1 Cup	dried cranberries

Preheat oven to 350°.

Cream shortening and the two sugars together.

Add eggs, vanilla, and boiling water. Mix.

Sift flour twice, once without the baking soda, once with the baking soda.

Add flour mixture to creamed mixture, mix well.

Add the oatmeal, mix well.

Add the chocolate chips, walnuts, and cranberries, mixing until well blended.

Drop by rounded teaspoons onto greased cookie sheet, 2 inches apart.

Bake for about 10 minutes. Watch closely so they don't over bake.

It is ok to pull them out of the oven while middle is still a little soft.

Let sit on baking pan for about 2 minutes, then move to a baking rack to finish cooling.

Mom's Chocolate Yeast Cake

This unusual chocolate cake is so chocolaty and unique, it is worth the extra effort. A nice dense chocolate cake.

1 Cup	margarine, or as mom used to call it, "oleo," softened
2 Cups	sugar
3	eggs
1 pkg.	dry yeast
¼ Cup	lukewarm water
6 oz.	bars of German sweet chocolate (1½ bars)
2 oz.	bittersweet baking chocolate (½ of a 4-oz. bar)
1 Cup	milk
3 Cups	flour
½ tsp.	salt
1 tsp.	baking soda
2 tsp.	vanilla
½ Cup	chopped nuts, if desired

My mom, Shirley. My hero, both in and out of the kitchen.

Preheat oven to 300°.

Cream margarine and sugar.

Beat in eggs 1 at a time.

Soften yeast in the water; add to creamed mixture.

Melt both chocolates in a double boiler. Or, use the microwave, but watch carefully and stir often.

Add the melted chocolate, milk, flour, salt, baking soda, vanilla, and chopped nuts to creamed mixture.

Beat by hand for 5 minutes.

Pour into a greased tube (angel food pan).

Level off in pan.

Cover. Chill for 6 hours or overnight.

Bake for 1 hour and 20 minutes.

Check with a toothpick to see if it comes out clean.

If not, keep baking and check every 5 minutes until done. Some pans are different diameters and it just depends on the pan size.

Once it tests done, let cool completely in the pan.

Loosen around edges and middle section with a butter knife.

Push the cake up from the bottom with the removable bottom.

Cut between the bottom pan and cake all the way around.

Remove from the bottom of pan.

Frost with your favorite chocolate frosting.

Sugar Cut-Out Cookies

Well, this is it! The recipe that launched my business.
Whether you want to start your own cookie business, or just want to make delicious cookies, this is the one that kept me in business for 13 years before my retirement.
Included are some fun designs.

½ Cup shortening
¼ Cup margarine
1 Cup sugar
2   jumbo eggs
1 tsp. vanilla
2½ Cups flour
1 tsp. baking powder
1 tsp. salt

Cream shortening, margarine, and sugar.
Mix in eggs and vanilla until well blended.
Add flour, baking powder, and salt. Mix well.
Wrap in plastic wrap.
Refrigerate for at least 4 hours, or overnight.

Preheat oven to 400°.
Roll dough ¼-⅓ inch thick on a floured surface, don't roll it too thin, you want a thick soft cookie.
Place on an ungreased baking sheet, or one lined with parchment paper.
Bake until top is just starting to get a very light brown, time is dependent on the size cutter used and thickness you rolled out dough to.
Let sit for about 3 minutes on baking tray.
Remove to a wire rack to cool completely before frosting (see my frosting recipe on page 203.)
This is a simple, basic recipe. What makes them special is how you decorate them.

My Vanilla Sugar Cookie Frosting

This is my base sugar cookie frosting. Many flavors can be added to make so many flavors.

2½ Tblsp.	margarine, softened
1½ Cups	powdered sugar
¾ tsp.	vanilla
1 Tblsp.	milk

Mix all ingredients well until thoroughly mixed. You want a nice spreading consistency.

Add a little more milk if too thick, a little more powdered sugar if too thin.

Use a non-serrated butter knife to spread the frosting.

If highlighting with another colored frosting, let dry for at least 24 hours before piping on the second color.

If highlighting with the same color, no need to let dry before highlighting.

Let dry for at least 24 hours before packaging or stacking cookies.

If you have highlighted the cookies, avoid stacking cookies on top of each other.

This is a soft frosting which crusts over, but does not become completely "hard" like some frostings.

Worth the extra effort. Here are some that I have done.

About Christine De Los Santos

I was born in Milwaukee, Wisconsin, into a very German family. I learned at an early age about food being our family's language of love. There were so many wonderful, inexpensive dishes on our table, so many baked goods made with love, and whatever was in season.

When I was a little older, I managed an apartment building. We had a wonderful mix of ethnic backgrounds in our building. You could tell that just by walking the apartment halls at dinner time. The wonderful smells of curry, Mexican, Asian, and Southern cooking, and oh so many others wafted through those hallways.

At that point, I was an expert at making Hamburger Helper, *but I could always bake…*

When I moved "Up North" a few years later, to the Fox Cities where I live now, I met the love of my life, Joel. After a nine-year courtship, we married and I gained four bonus children to go along with my two sons. We became a family of three sons and three daughters (but no maid named Alice).

I have a degree in computer programming and worked in that field for almost twenty years. It never really was my passion, but I was good at it, and I met some wonderful people in the process. The one thing that I did enjoy was bringing my home-baked treats to my co-workers…*that* was my passion.

When my last programming job was eliminated, I made the decision to start my retirement from computer programming and began following my passion for cookie baking. That was in 2003, when I started my business, Happy Cookies, named by our oldest granddaughter, Alex, who always called birthday cakes "Happy Cakes," because of the "Happy Birthday" song.

I have been given the honor of baking cookies for many weddings, showers, birthdays, holidays, and any other special day that needed to be made just a little more…Happy.

Happily, my cookies began to become a tradition for the families of many brides for whose weddings I baked. I also spent many years baking cookies for our Fox Cities Performing Arts Center, whenever they had a large show.

Baking for my customers has always been an honor. The opportunity to bake for some of my favorite celebrities was an unexpected surprise, especially when *Woman's Day* magazine flew me out to Los Angeles to bring cookies to the cast of *Hot in Cleveland*, which included my favorite celebrity, Betty White. I have also had the honor of making cookies for my favorite singer, Martina McBride, comedian and actor Brad Garrett, a number of Packers players' wives, and some of our local television news personalities.

More than 10 years ago, I began cooking and baking on TV, on two local shows named *Good Day Wisconsin*, and later on *Living with Amy*. The folks on the shows began referring to me as "The Happy Cookie Lady," and the name stuck.

After having some physical issues with my knees—standing so much running the business and baking—I made the difficult decision to retire from baking for a living in 2016, so I could work on this cookbook, and spend more time with family.

Now that it is finished, there will be more time for the gardens, more time for my wonderful hubby, more time for our 8 grandchildren and other family members.

I still get to cook and bake on TV, when they need me to. It is always fun!

Happy Cooking!

Made in the USA
Monee, IL
20 December 2024